MAKING Vinyl, Plastic, & Rubber

Handbags

Sewing Stylish Projects from Unusual Materials

GLOUCESTER MASSACHUSETTS

QUARRY BOOKS

Ellen Goldstein-Lynch, Nicole Malone, and Sarah Mullins
of the Accessories Design Department at the Fashion Institute of Technology

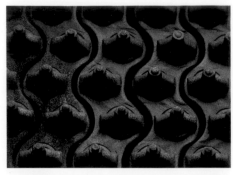

Contents

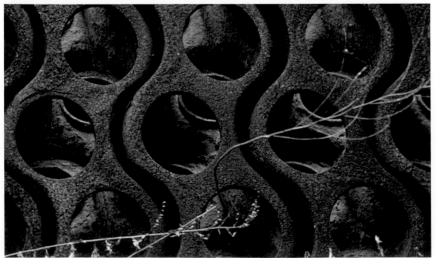

Introduction

In 2002, when Quarry Books approached us about doing a book on making handbags, we were elated. Why? Because of all the people in the world that they could have approached to do this project, the three of us are crazy for handbags (optimum word here is *crazy*). Little did we know that the response to our first book, *Making Handbags*, would be so enormous that Rockport would approach us two years later for a sequel, but this time to author a book on handbags made only with leather. Just as before, the book, *Making Leather Handbags and Other Stylish Accessories*, took off with the help of other talented craftspeople around the world.

This time we had an even greater challenge: to produce a book using unusual materials and fabrications such as vinyl, plastic, and even rubber. These are materials that you would find as floor mats, car mats, inner tubes, upholstery vinyl, or even gum wrappers. As in previous books, one of our goals was to challenge our students to use their creativity by using our patterns in their own special way. The results are right behind this page and, if we must say so, they are unbelievably spectacular. So why have we taken you down memory lane?

Because for the past four years our publisher has allowed us to do what we do best—to create one-of-a-kind and somewhat crazy designs of the best accessory in a woman's wardrobe. We truly are "bag ladies" and we hope that you will be just as inspired by these projects as we were while creating them.

If this is your first experience with us, hold on to your hat for the ride of your creative life. And if this is your third experience, you will not be disappointed. In fact, we think you will be quite excited by how versatile, weatherproof, sturdy, and plain-old fun these materials are to work with. So, without further ado, turn on the lights in your studio, get your sewing machine ready, clear away the cobwebs on your worktable, and turn the page. Your next step toward a more dramatic, electrified, and glamorous collection of handbags awaits you.

Happy sewing!

ELLEN GOLDSTEIN-LYNCH
NICOLE MALONE
AND SARAH MULLINS,
FASHION INSTITUTE OF TECHNOLOGY

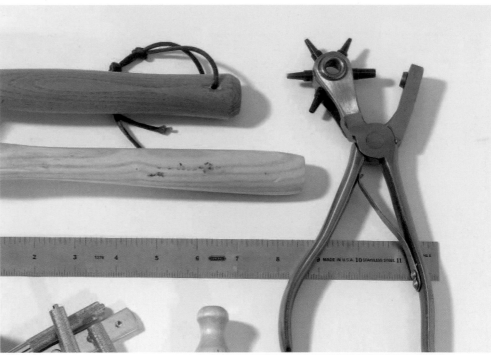

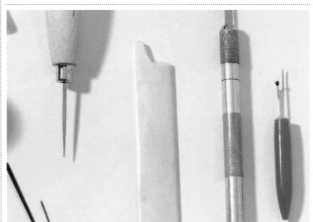

Section One: Getting Started

Supplies and Tools

No one says that you need to have a fully equipped sewing room or studio to make handbags and small fashion accessories. All you need are a few basic supplies and, of course, your imagination.

PUNCHING A HOLE

Place the punch over the material and hit with mallet.

You definitely need a **sewing machine**—the specific type doesn't matter, as long as you are comfortable working with it. The machine should have an automatic *reverse-stitch* selector and *interchangeable presser-foot attachments*. Some of the best machines are the old Singer treadles, but the newer models work just as well. You can also use the machines with a computer memory for embroidery and embellishment detailing as well as regular sewing. Although most projects featured in this book can be completed on a home sewing machine, if you want to purchase a commercial sewing machine, these machines are available for home use. Just make sure that whatever machine you do use is well oiled and maintained. A sluggish machine is a hungry machine and will tend to "eat" your fabric.

Presser-foot attachments are available for most machines. Think in terms of zipper, gauge, and binding attachments. Teflon ones are appropriate for working on vinyl, plastic, and coated fabrics and will fit most home sewing machines. Do your homework, and make the investment. You never know when your imagination will call on your "feet" to do the work.

Find a **flat surface** to work on. A folding table, kitchen table, or sewing table is perfect. Make sure the table is secure and not wobbly. Also make sure that the surface is clean. You don't want food, grease, or grime to get on your projects.

When cutting vinyl, plastic, and other coated fabrics, be sure to use a **cutting board**. The board not only

TOOLS

A   needle-nose pliers
B   mallet
C   hammer
D   rotary cutter
E   metal ruler
F   rotary hole punch
G   69 bonded nylon thread
H   rivet- and snap-setter kit
I   Top: gauge foot
     Middle: Teflon foot
     Bottom: zipper foot

J   hole punch
K   oval punch
L   rivet setter
M   binder clips
N   grommet setter
O   awl
P   bone folder
Q   craft knife
R   seam ripper
S   magnetic snap and washers
T   turn lock

U   buckle
V   O-ring; D-ring
W   grommet and washer
X   rivet
Y   collar pin set
Z   lacing needle

SETTING A RIVET

(a) Assemble the materials and punch hole.

(b) Place rivet post through hole. Push rivet cap onto post. Hammer rivet setter over cap to set.

(c) Remove setter and check that rivet is securely set.

protects your table, but also provides a stable surface for cutting. Many boards are "self-healing," which means they mend any cut marks themselves. Just make sure that the cutting board you use has a smooth surface.

Lighting is critical. Without proper lighting your eyes will play tricks on you. Natural light is the best, but if you don't have that don't worry. Just make sure you have sufficient light when sewing.

When using craft or fabric glue, be sure to work near a window or with a fan on, to ensure **proper ventilation**. If you start to get a headache from the glue, stop working immediately and get some fresh air.

Rubber cement, also known as contact cement, is essential for most vinyl and plastic handbag and fashion accessories projects. When working with two pieces of material, you need to cement both pieces, let the cement dry, and then put the pieces together.

Before getting started, though, be sure your cement is relatively new (less than six months old), read the instructions for using it (is proper ventilation, heat, or cold needed?), and have an extra jar available just in case. Also, be sure to use newspaper on your gluing surface to prevent excess glue from getting onto your table and, ultimately, onto your project. *Note: Latex adhesive works well on vinyl and plastics, as do other basic types of glues. Any adhesive you choose should always be tested on a scrap piece of vinyl, plastic, or coated fabric prior to starting your project. Consult your local hardware store to learn which adhesives are compatible with your handbag materials.*

A craftsperson can never have too many pairs of **scissors**. Just make sure they are sharp enough to cut through vinyl.

You may even want to have one pair reserved strictly for cutting vinyl and another strictly for fabric. Also important is that the scissors fit comfortably in your hand. Various ergonomically correct scissors are on the market, so do your homework and shop around. A **rotary cutter** is also great for cutting both vinyl and fabric, so make sure you have one of those in your sewing box as well.

Pinking shears are great for decorative detailing, but make sure they are sharp. Dull pinking shears won't even cut butter.

Utility and craft knives are ideal for cutting heavy vinyl and plastics. Again, just make sure the blade is sharp.

To get a smooth folded edge on vinyl or plastic, you need to use a **bone folder**. The original bone folders were made of whalebone, but the newer models are made of plastic. Also, some bone folders are strictly for left- or right-handed people. Be sure to get the one that's right for you. Check your craft catalogs and resource lists for more information.

We recommend that you use a strong **thread**, whichever type works best on your machine. Nylon thread works well with vinyl and plastic, so you might want to consider using it. For some projects you'll need contrasting colors, so stock up on your favorites. Also, remember to buy embroidery thread for adding contrasting details to your projects; you can use either pearl cotton or embroidery floss.

Most machines do come with **needles**, and in some cases you can buy a variety pack. Make sure that you have a range of different sizes for stitching different fabrics and that you invest in leather needles for sewing different weights of vinyl and plastic.

SETTING A GROMMET

(a) After hole is punched, place grommet through the hole from the front. Place grommet on the anvil front-side down. Place washer over grommet on the back side.

(b) Place setter into the grommet and hit with mallet.

(c) Remove setter and check that grommet is securely set.

ADDING A COLLAR PIN

(A) After punching a hole, place the screw through the hole from the bottom.

(B) Screw collar pin on.

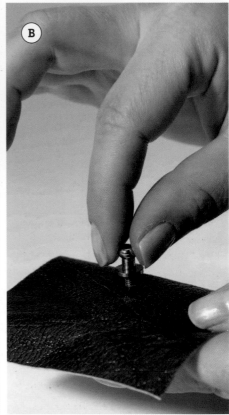

Hand-sewing needles are also essential, so make sure you have a variety of those on hand as well. If you are going to be doing embroidery, use an **embroidery needle**. For beading on vinyl or plastic, use a **glover's needle**; for lacing on vinyl or plastic, use a **lacing needle**. Remember to change your needles regularly. Like scissors, they tend to get dull with repeated use.

You'll need **straight pins** for pinning lining and fabric in place. Whether you buy them on a wheel or in a box, make sure you have enough on hand. Just remember that you can't use straight pins on vinyl, plastic, or leather because they will leave marks.

Binder, or **bulldog**, **clips** are those black metal clips used to hold papers together. They are also great for holding several pieces of vinyl or plastic together, making the sewing process a lot easier. It's like having an extra pair of hands. The ¾" to 1" (1.9 to 2.5 cm) size is perfect for most projects. You can buy them individually or in packages, in black or in a variety of colors at office supply stores.

Double-sided craft tape is great for turning in edges of coated fabric, vinyl, or plastic. It's also perfect for temporarily adhering pieces before sewing, rather than using glue and risk having it seep into the coated

fabric or vinyl and staining it. The ¼" (6 mm) size is the best to use.

Masking tape, that "old reliable," comes in handy for almost any craft project, especially for holding the vinyl or plastic in place while you cut out your patterns. Keep several rolls on hand.

Metal rulers are the best type of ruler to use when working with vinyl, plastic, or rubber. You get a more accurate cut when you use them to guide your cutting, and in the long run, they will save your fingers.

Snap-, **grommet-**, **eyelet-**, and **rivet-setting kits**, along with a **rotary** or **handheld leather hole punch**, are also important when doing vinyl, plastic, or rubber projects. Snaps, grommets, and rivets add decorative pizzazz to your designs and really jazz up a collection, and a rotary punch makes it easier to make holes in the vinyl, plastic, or rubber. If you're a serious craftsperson, you need these items in your supply inventory.

For making holes in patterns and in your material, you will need a really sharp **awl**. It looks like an old-fashioned ice pick with a wooden bulbous handle. The craftsperson's version has a fine point, which is perfect for these projects. Wider points, on the other hand, are not effective in penetrating patterns or material.

Also, don't forget to have a supply of **fabric-marking pens and pencils** and **silver pens** on hand for transferring pattern pieces onto your fabric, vinyl, plastic, or rubber.

Other optional tools that can make crafting life easier are a pair of needle-nose pliers, a handsaw, and a rawhide **mallet** or **hammer**. In the back of this book you will find an extensive resource list of suppliers of materials and tools. We suggest that you refer to this section when updating your supply inventory. Many of the resources have websites and catalogs.

With supplies in hand, you are equipped with the crafting essentials necessary for creating the projects in this book. So, what are you waiting for? Grab your supplies, label them, and put them in handy carriers or in an easily accessible place. Make sure that the tools are sharpened, your sewing machine is well oiled, and the pieces to your kits are all there. Before you start on that first project, though, check out the next chapter, the ABCs of Vinyl, Plastic, Rubber, and Coated Fabrics.

USING A LEATHER PUNCH

(A) Place oval punch in desired location and hit with mallet.

(B) Remove punch.

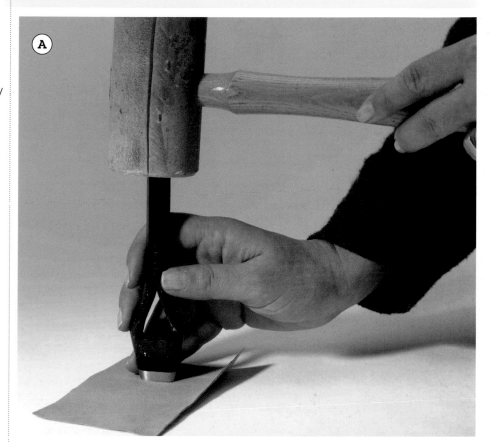

ABCs of Vinyl, Plastic, Rubber, and Coated Fabrics

The fabrics used in this book represent a variety of unusual materials not traditionally associated with the construction of handbags and fashion accessories. But, who is to say you can't use them? We welcomed this challenge not just because the materials are unusual but because they are bright, bold, and textural. Plus they create a truly one-of-a-kind accessory.

As with every type of material you select, test it first! Make sure that your machine can handle the thickness of the material or the resistance of the material to the machine bed. Test the glues as well to make sure that the glue you use doesn't eat away at the fabric or its lining.

Most unusual fabrics can also be found in unexpected places rather than a fabric store. Check tag sales and flea markets for coated fabrics and plastics, noting the tablecloths of the '30s, '40s, and '50s were made of waterproof oilcloth. Check hardware stores and the mega home supply stores for shower curtains, rubber mats, and car upholstery materials. And, check thrift stores for old bags and other recyclable materials. Using these materials gives you a creative edge that is all your own.

What Is a Coated Fabric?

Coated fabrics have a layer of lacquer, varnish, propylene, rubber, or plastic resin on either one side or both sides. This layer acts as a water repellent and can be used on cotton, silk, and oilcloth.

What Is Impregnated Fabric?

Impregnated fabrics feature a coating that has been infused into the weave of the fabric. This allows the fabric to become waterproof. Examples of impregnated fabrics include cotton canvas or oilcloth.

What Is Vinyl?

Vinyl is a general term used for a material made of polymers or polyvinyl chloride. Vinyl comes in a variety of colors and textures. It is extremely durable and, in some cases, can be handled the same way as leather.

What Is Urethane?

Urethane is another type of material that can be used for these projects. Urethanes can also be embossed to look like leathers, snakeskins, and other exotic skins.

What Is Rubber?

Rubber is a manufactured fiber in which the fiber-forming substance is composed of natural or synthetic rubber. Rubberized fabric takes on the same characteristics as an impregnated fabric. There is a wide range of rubberized fabrics, including cotton, rainwear, and shower curtains. Many of these rubberized fabrics have great prints and patterns that can be easily applied to our projects.

What Is Plastic?

The type of plastic used for our projects is called thermoplastic. This type of plastic resin can be formed into fibers and then fabricated into cloth. A clear plastic tablecloth or shower curtain would be made of this type of material. Be careful when working with plastics because they have a tendency to be more brittle and less pliable than urethanes or coated fabrics.

Embellishments, Trims, and Decorative Techniques

Embellishments can either make or break your design. They add character to your creation. They express you and your personality. They are what separate your design from anyone else's. What's more, they tie your collection of accessories together, making them unique.

Selecting the right type of trim or embellishment is up to you. Whatever suits your mood, your outfit, and your attitude is ultimately the right one to use. So, in keeping with the adage that change is good, here are a few trims and embellishments that can add character to your creations.

Appliqués come in various colors, sizes, and shapes. Embroidered patches, flowers, initials, and animals all make great additions to the outside of your handbags and small fashion accessories. You will find that pieces of contrasting vinyl or coated fabrics and surface appliqués of initials on solid vinyl, rubber, or plastic also make a striking statement.

While we're talking appliqué don't forget **reverse appliqué**, which adds color and shape through cutwork. This type of appliqué gives your design personality. Remember to experiment with exotic skins for appliqué. They are a major plus in this category of trims and embellishments!

Trapunto can help give your collection a three-dimensional look by padding your design motif. By topstitching your designs with contrasting threads, you can add a touch of whimsy or stylish sophistication to a small fashion accessory or handbag silhouette.

You can never have enough **baubles**, **bangles**, and **beads**, especially when you look at all of the beaded embellishments on the bags in the stores. They come in various colors, sizes, and shapes, and can be hand sewn to the handbag material by using a glover's needle. If it's gemstones you are looking to add, purchase a Be-Dazzler Stud & Rhinestone Setting Machine or a stone-setting kit. Whatever you choose, choose it wisely. You're creating a fashion statement that just may make your designs the talk of the neighborhood.

Buttons are used as closures as well as embellishments. They come

in various colors, shapes, and sizes, so you can search for just the right ones for your projects. Also, remember that some catalogs and stores specialize in antique and collectible buttons, if that's what you're into.

Embroidery stitches such as satin, French knot, couch, and leaf stitches are just a few of the types of stitches you can use to add dimension and interest to your projects. Use these decorative stitches by themselves or with embroidery appliqués for added impact. Just remember that when applying this technique to vinyl, plastic, or coated fabric you need to use an embroidery needle.

For that straight-from-the-garden look, **silk flowers** can be found at most craft stores and floral suppliers. Use one as a focal point on the flap of a bag or handle. Shop for just the right one. Most craft stores have a huge garden blooming year-round.

Fringe and **tassels** make amazing trims because they are three-dimensional and add move-ment. So, if you're looking for that special something that catches people's eyes when you walk, consider adding little bit of fringe or a tassel. Just remember not to overdo it so much that it gets in your way.

Grommets, **eyelets**, **snaps**, and **studs**, besides serving as functional embellishments, can also be used as trims. Cover the entire front of the bag or small fashion accessory with grommets and eyelets for a military look. Use snaps to attach appliqués to your collection so you can change the appliqué with your outfit. Studs are fabulous for making that urban statement really stand out.

Use old pieces of **jewelry**, such as necklaces and pins, to accent your collections. These can be either permanently affixed or changed with your outfit. It's always fun to go scavenging through flea markets and antique stores for just the right piece. Also, don't forget that necklaces and bracelets make great handles as well.

Lace and **lace appliqué** add sophistication and worldliness to any creation. Whether you use lace pieces, small Battenburg flowers, or ruffled lace strips, the end result is breathtakingly elegant.

Lacing is a technique that works beautifully on the raw edges of vinyl or rubber. It adds an urban or rustic look that is perfect for the fashion-current designer.

Use **fabric paint, acrylic paint, luma dyes, and leather edge dye** to add a bit of whimsy to your bags and small fashion accessories. Experiment with a small piece of material to make sure that the paint doesn't crack or peel.

Quilting and **smocking** are tech-niques that can be used to enhance your collection three-dimensionally. Again, experiment with the tech-niques before using them on your designs. You might consider smock-ing a flap or quilting a pocket for greater design impact.

Decorative ribbons can create a three-dimensional effect that sepa-rates your creations from others. Use ribbons as part of your embroidery, creating flowers or leaves on pock-ets, flaps, or handles.

Go shopping at the hardware store and in thrift shops for different and interesting pieces of **hardware** to attach to your creations. Consider decorative drawer pulls for handles, wooden knobs and dowels, or even some funky metal tubing and wash-ers. You never know what you will find. A hardware store can be a treasure trove of interesting finds, so use your imagination.

Topstitching, like embroidery stitching, adds detail to your creations. Use a contrasting color of thread when topstitching for a dramatic effect.

Laying Out and Cutting Your Patterns and Sewing

You've just come back from your material-buying spree with the most fabulous colors and patterns. You've decided on the first project, and you've coordinated your purchases to that favorite dress hanging in your closet. Before you do anything, you need to follow these simple instructions to ensure that your patterns fit your materials and are laid out properly:

NOTES:

For additional help with specific sewing terms, see the Glossary on page 123. For information on supplies and tools, see Resources on page 125.

01
Check to make sure that your tabletop is covered with a cutting board or cutting surface. This will prevent you from ruining your table.

02
When cutting out patterns, don't cut the vinyl, heavy plastic, rubber, or urethane with scissors. Instead use a utility knife, craft knife, or rotary cutter and a straightedge such as a metal ruler. When cutting around curved edges, use the pattern as your guide. On lighter-weight materials you can use scissors, but be careful. When in doubt, use a rotary cutter to be safe.

03
Be extra careful when using tape to hold your patterns down on your materials. Test the material first. Some tapes may remove the finish and leave a mark.

04
Using a Teflon foot for your projects can and will be a lifesaver. The Teflon coating allows the materials to move effortlessly through the feeder portion of the sewing machine. Although you can sew some coated fabrics without a Teflon foot, why make your sewing experience difficult? Teflon foot attachments are available at most sewing supply stores and fit most home sewing machines.

05
A gauge foot can act as your sewing guide: It allows you to sew in a straight line without causing your material to pucker or waiver. A zipper foot, on the other hand, allows you to sew close to zipper teeth or piping.

Now it's on to the wonderful world of vinyl, plastic, rubber, and coated fabric handbags and small fashion accessories projects—or, better yet, the realm of your imagination!

Section Two: Projects

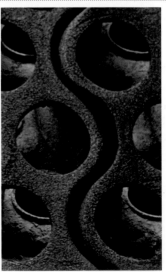

Candy Wrapper Bling Belt

Interesting and colorful belts have become one of the hottest accessories, and this one is no exception. This straight belt features a rhinestone buckle and is covered all around with lively candy wrapper graphics! Here's a stylish, low-calorie way to grace your waist with your favorite confections. And don't just settle for one; make a few, because you're sure to get requests from all your friends.

Getting Started

Measure the width for the belt opening in the belt buckle. Subtract ⅛" (3 mm) from this measurement and cut the two strips of vinyl (one for filler, one for lining) this width by the length you need to fit around your waist, plus 2" (5.1 cm) or so to pass through the buckle. Use a tape measure around your favorite pair of pants, or take measurements from a belt that you already own. Then, using a utility knife or scissors, cut a piece of clear vinyl ½" (1.3 cm) longer and wider all around than the size of the two vinyl strips.

MATERIALS

two strips of medium-weight vinyl (one for filler, one for lining), each long enough to make a belt in your size, and the proper width to fit your buckle

one strip of clear, lightweight vinyl, ½" (1.3 cm) longer and wider than previous vinyl strips

candy wrappers (enough to cover belt)

one utility/military buckle

double-sided craft tape (⅛" to ¼" [3 to 6 mm] wide)

multipurpose craft glue

rubber cement

matching thread for machine sewing

TOOLS

utility or craft knife or scissors

cutting mat (if using utility knife)

bone folder

24" (61 cm) or longer metal ruler

binder clips

scissors

MACHINERY

home sewing machine with a ⅛" (3 mm) gauge foot

Instructions

01

Lay out the candy wrappers in a flat fashion all along the length of the vinyl for belt filler, with the edges slightly over-lapping each other. Glue in place with craft glue, letting the ends extend beyond the edge of the belt. With scissors, trim the excess candy wrappers ⅜" (1 cm) beyond the edge of the belt filler.

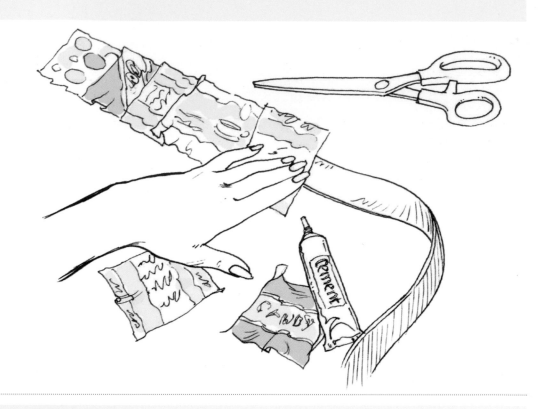

02

Cement the back sides of additional candy wrap-pers. After the glue has dried, crinkle the wrappers into desired shapes and glue onto the flat candy wrappers already attached to the belt, letting some edges extend beyond the edge of the filler. After the length of the belt is covered, trim the edges at the same ⅜" (1 cm) allowance beyond the edge as previously done.

03

Using rubber cement, glue ⅜" (1 cm) of the inside edge of the wrappers to the inner edge of the filler. Let dry, then adhere by turning onto the inside of the belt using a bone folder.

04

Adhere double-sided tape to the outer edge of the clear vinyl (on the inside of the belt), then turn onto the inside (filler side) of the belt all around. Pinch together the corners and clip with scissors.

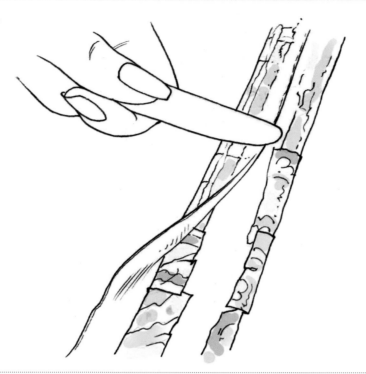

05

Use double-sided tape or rubber cement to attach vinyl lining to inside of belt.

06

Topstitch ⅛" (3 mm) all around the edge of the belt, catching the lining.

07

Insert the end of the belt into the buckle and wear with your favorite outfit!

Diamond Plate Shopping Tote

Rubber floor mats are not just for the floor anymore. Use them to create a striking tote bag instead. High-tech, floral, or geometric designs create a signature pattern that will be admired by friends and family for years to come. Our tote is in a diamond plate pattern accented with an orange button elastic. Find a fun button and hand sew it on the front of your bag for a unique closure or rivet a pocket onto the front or back of the bag in a contrasting color or pattern for extra storage. Any way you slice it, our floor mat tote is not only sturdy, practical, funky, and gorgeous—it's a conversation starter.

Getting Started

Trace the shopping tote bag patterns with a marking pen and cut out all pieces with scissors. Alternatively, use a weight or loops of tape to hold the pattern down and cut the matting with a knife.

Line up the metal ruler along the straight edges of the patterns while cutting out the pattern pieces with a utility knife. When cutting rounded edges, simply use the edge of the pattern as a guide. Always cut on a cutting board to prevent marring your tabletop.

Transfer all hole locations from the pattern onto the matting with a marking pen.

MATERIALS

one 18" x 30" (46 x 76 cm) piece of diamond plate matting, ⁵⁄₃₂" (4 mm) thick

twenty-eight ⁵⁄₁₆" (8 mm) -long rivets

two ½" (15 mm) -long rivets

12" (30.5 cm) -long, round elastic cord

TOOLS

rotary or handheld hole punch, size #2 (⅛" or 3 mm)

cardboard, 8-oz. leather, or wood for punching board (if using handheld hole puch)

rivet-setting kit

utility knife

12" (30.5 cm) and 24" (61 cm) metal rulers

masking tape and/or pattern weights

rawhide mallet or hammer

gel roller marking pen

scissors

one piece of 13" x 2" x 4" (33 x 15 x 10 cm) wood or similar material

pattern (see page 92)

Instructions

01

Punch out all holes with a rotary or handheld size #2 punch as noted on the pattern.

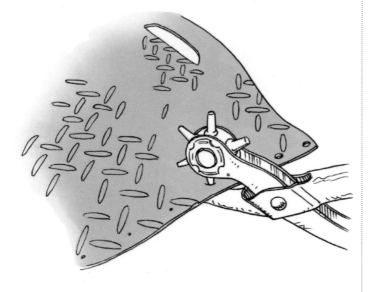

02

Cut out a 1" (2.5 cm) circle for the front button. Punch a hole in the center using a #2 punch and rivet the button to the front of the bag with a $\frac{5}{16}$" (8 mm) -long rivet.

03

Use a rivet-setting kit to set eight $\frac{5}{16}$" (8 mm) rivets along one side of the bag, overlapping the front section onto the back. Leave the bottom holes open until step 6.

04

Repeat step 3 for the other side, overlapping the front section onto the back and leaving the bottom holes open until step 6.

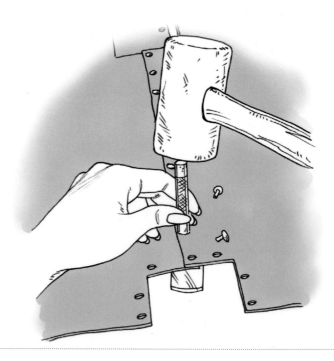

05

Turn the bag upside down and use the 13" x 2" x 4" (33 x 15 x 10 cm) piece of wood as a stand to set seven ⁵⁄₁₆" (8 mm) rivets along the bottom of the bag. Overlap the front section onto the back and leave the holes on both ends open until step 6.

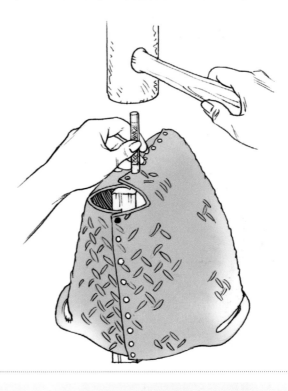

06

Line up the center bottom holes of the side with the center end holes of the bottom and set one ½" (15 mm) rivet through all four layers. Set two ⁵⁄₁₆" (8 mm) rivets through the two remaining holes. Repeat for the other side.

07

Tie a knot in the end of the round elastic cord and pull the loop through the hole at the center top of the back of the bag for the closure.

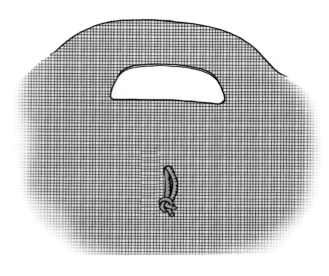

Aloha Vanity Case

The last thing you need when you travel is a makeup case that is heavy, dull, and boring. This Hawaiian-themed cosmetic case allows for easy airport inspection and quick lipstick selection, and is full of festive personal style. Made of printed clear vinyl shower curtain material with contrasting colored zipper and handle, this showstopper is sure to please even the most discerning tastes. Make several in assorted sizes to hold lingerie, jewelry, or shoes.

MATERIALS

shower curtain or 24" x 18" (61 x 45.7 cm) piece of lightweight to medium-weight vinyl with a fun print

11" x 9" (27.9 x 22.9 cm) piece of medium- to heavy-weight vinyl (we used a plastic floor runner)

13" (33 cm) zipper

thread for machine sewing

TOOLS

utility knife

12" (30.5 cm) metal ruler

cutting mat

double-sided craft tape (¼" [6 mm] wide)

binder clips

scissors

pinking shears

masking tape

patterns (see page 112)

MACHINERY

home sewing machine with a Teflon foot and ⅛" (3 mm) gauge foot

Getting Started

When cutting all pieces for this project, use loops of tape to hold down the pattern and cut the vinyl with a knife.

Line up the metal ruler along the straight edges of the patterns while cutting out the material with a utility knife. When cutting rounded edges, simply use the edge of your pattern as a guide. *Note: Be sure to cut on a proper surface.*

Cut out all pieces for the vanity case from patterns as labeled. Also cut out an 11" x 3" (27.9 x 7.6 cm) strip from a shower curtain (or vinyl) for the handle and an 11" x ⅝" (27.9 x 1.6 cm) strip from heavier vinyl (or plastic floor runner).

Instructions

01

Using masking tape, attach the outer edges of the zipper to the back side of the top-zip pieces (along the straight edges). Be sure to keep the tape outside the ⅛" (3 mm) stitch line. Flip the pieces over to their good sides and topstitch along the edge of the vinyl on both sides of the zipper, ⅛" (3 mm) away from the edge, using a gauge foot.

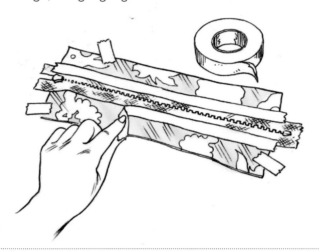

02

Using binder clips, clip and sew an end of the top-zip piece to a gusset piece using a ⅜" (1 cm) seam allowance, good sides facing each other, back tacking at the beginning and end of the stitch line. Repeat for the other side with the other gusset. Pull back the gusset from the top-zip piece and topstitch on the top edges of the gussets, ⅛" (3 mm) away from the seam, using a gauge foot.

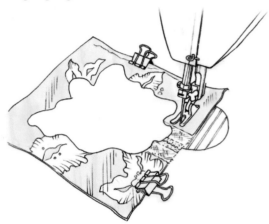

03

Using binder clips, clip and sew the bottom edges of the front and back pieces together using a ⅜" (1 cm) seam allowance, good sides facing each other. Press the seams open and topstitch on either side of the seam, using the ⅛" (3 mm) gauge foot.

04

Center the bottom reinforcement piece on the outside bottom seam of the front and back pieces. Temporarily hold in place with masking tape on the outer edges. Topstitch all around the bottom reinforcement piece, using the gauge foot, removing the tape as you sew.

05

To make the handle, fold both long ends of the 11" x 3" (27.9 x 7.6 cm) handle strip in toward the center 1" (2.5 cm) from both sides, overlapping in the center to create a 1" (2.5 cm)-wide handle. Keep the folded ends down with binder clips. Topstitch along each long side using the gauge foot. Then place the 11" x ⅝" (27.9 x 1.6 cm) strip down the center of the handle, temporarily holding it in place with masking tape. Topstitch along each long side of the ⅝" (1.6 cm) strip using the gauge foot, removing the tape as you sew.

06

Using binder clips, clip the top-zip/gusset piece to the front/bottom/back piece all around, good sides facing each other, being sure to match up at all center notches. Place each end of the handle at the center top notches of the front and back pieces, and place the raw edge of the short ends of the handle at the center top edges of the bag. The handle should be inside the bag, with the good side of the handle facing the good side of the bag. Make sure you leave the zipper open. Using the Teflon foot, sew all around using a ⅜" (1 cm) seam allowance. Trim the excess seam allowance with pinking shears. Turn the bag right side out.

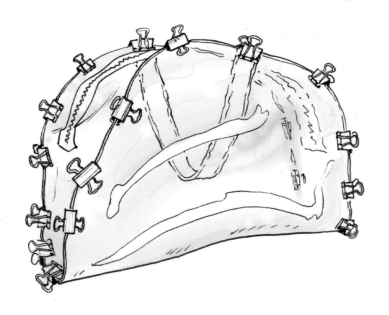

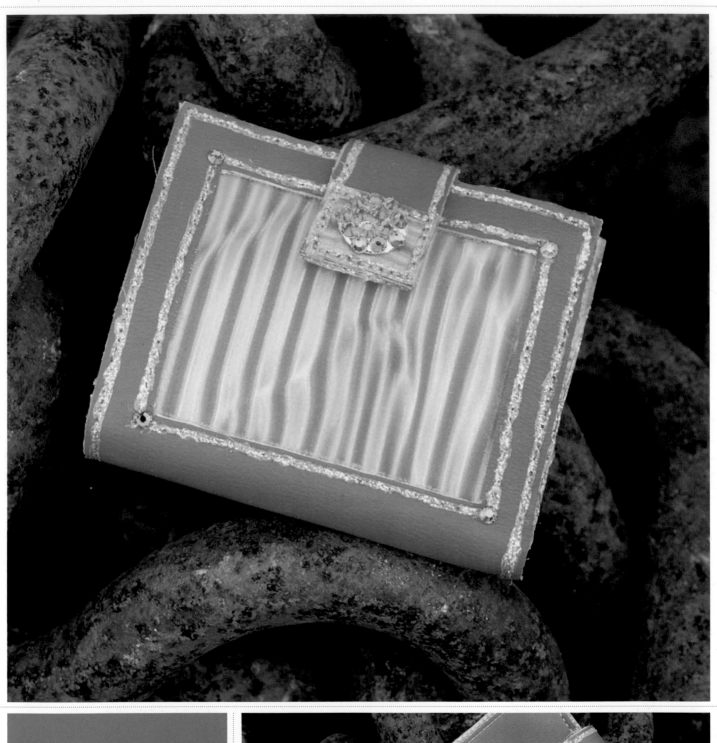

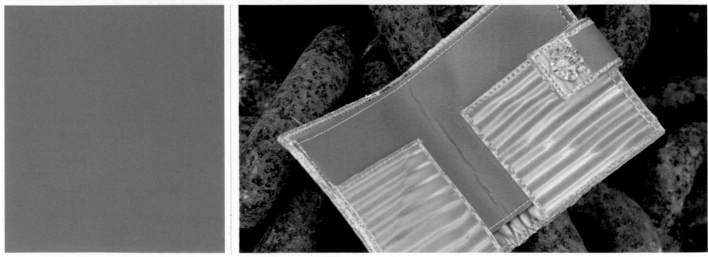

Holographic Techno-Wallet

Glam, glitz, and pizzazz sum up the Holographic Techno-Wallet. With gold and jeweled accents, this wallet is a natural accessory for anyone who's feeling a little dull and needs some eye candy! Instead of the holographic vinyl, substitute faux snake-skin or faux leather for a more sophisticated rendition.

Getting Started

When cutting all pieces for this project, use loops of tape to hold down the pattern and cut the vinyl with a knife.

Line up the metal ruler along the straight edges of the patterns while cutting out the material with a utility knife. *Note: Be sure to cut on a proper surface.*

Cement the interior side pockets together, good sides outward (holographic on the front, thin vinyl as lining). Cement the interior bill pocket to the lining, good sides outward. Cement the outside and lining tabs together, good sides outward.

MATERIALS

9" x 9" (22.9 x 22.9 cm) piece of upholstery-weight vinyl (for outside of wallet, front of interior bill pocket, and tab)

11" x 9" (27.9 x 22.9 cm) piece of lightweight vinyl/PVC (for wallet and pocket linings)

9" x 8" (22.9 x 20.3 cm) piece of thin holographic plastic/vinyl

snap set

approximately twenty-one rhinestones

rubber cement

epoxy glue

thread for machine sewing

TOOLS

rotary or handheld hole punch, size #2 (⅛" [3 mm])

cardboard, 8 oz. leather, or wood for punching board (if using handheld hole punch)

double-sided craft tape (¼" [6 mm] wide)

snap-setting kit

utility or craft knife

12" (30.5 cm) metal ruler

masking tape and/or pattern weights

rawhide mallet or hammer

awl

binder clips

fabric glitter pen

patterns (see page 103)

MACHINERY

home sewing machine with a ¹⁄₁₆" (1.6 mm) gauge foot

Instructions

01

Place holographic vinyl behind the front/back of the wallet cutouts, matching up the outer edges. Secure in place with double-sided tape. Using a ⅟₁₆" (1.6 mm) gauge foot, topstitch all around the cutouts.

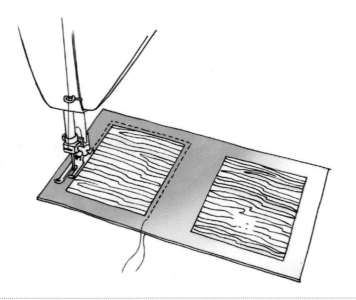

02

Using a ⅟₁₆" (1.6 mm) gauge foot, topstitch the top edge of the interior side pockets.

03

Using double-sided tape, attach the holographic detail to the front of the tab. Using a ⅟₁₆" (1.6 mm) gauge foot, topstitch all around the edge of the tab, then up the inner edge of the detail. Transfer the snap marking to the front of the wallet and front of the tab with an awl.

04

Punch holes through the front of the tab and front of the wallet with a hole punch.

05

Set the snap through the front of the tab and front of the wallet with a snap-setting tool.

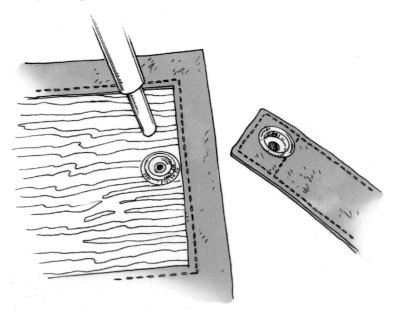

06

Using a ⅟₁₆" (1.6 mm) gauge foot, topstitch the bottom edge of the interior bill pocket. Then topstitch the inside of the interior side pockets to the interior bill pocket as noted on the pattern.

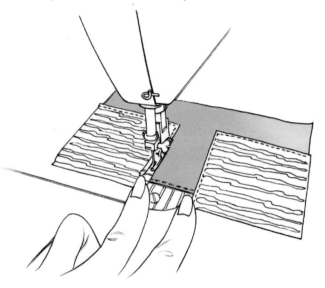

07

Cement the wallet front/back piece to the lining piece, inserting the tab between the layers where noted on the pattern.

08

Using double-sided tape and binder clips, attach the interior bill pocket to the wallet, matching up the edges all around. *Note: The interior is shorter than the outside, so you must curve it in order to match it up.*

Topstitch all around the outer edge using a ⅟₁₆" (1.6 mm) gauge foot.

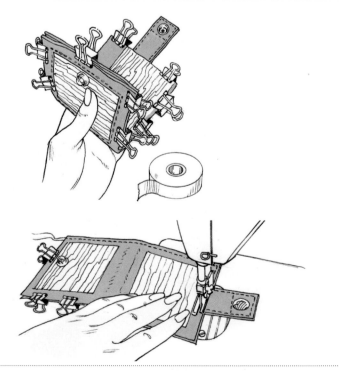

09

If desired, embellish your wallet by using a fabric glitter pen all along the topstitching, and apply rhinestones to the snap and other parts of the wallet using epoxy glue.

Retro Sparkle Messenger Bag

Nothing makes you feel more like a million dollars than something sparkling and white. And, if it can't be diamonds and jewels, the next best thing is this fabulous iridescent vinyl messenger bag. It is a perfect splash of sheen for work or play. The bag sports a seat-belt strap for a comfortable shoulder fit along with a magnetic closure. Use an accent color to attract attention like our emerald green iridescent vinyl and create a collection of gems sure to sparkle up any wardrobe.

MATERIALS

24" x 36" (61 x 91.4 cm) piece of vinyl

36" x 36" (91.4 x 91.4 cm) piece of ripstop nylon fabric lining

6" x 12" (15.2 x 30.5 cm) piece of appliqué vinyl

one sew-in magnetic snap

58" (147.3 cm) length of 1½" (3.8 cm) webbing

two 1½" (3.8 cm) metal D-rings

matching thread for machine sewing

acrylic paint to match appliqué piece

TOOLS

utility or craft knife

12" (30.5 cm) and 24" (61 cm) metal rulers

masking tape and/or pattern weights

rubber cement or fabric glue

double-sided craft tape (¼" [6 mm] wide)

binder clips

marking pen

scissors

straight pins

patterns (see page 109)

MACHINERY

home sewing machine with a Teflon foot and zipper foot

Getting Started

Trace the messenger bag patterns with a marking pen and cut out all vinyl pieces with scissors or use a weight or loops of tape to hold down the patterns and cut with a knife.

Line up the metal ruler along the straight edges of the patterns while cutting out the vinyl pieces with a utility knife. When cutting rounded edges, simply use the edge of your pattern as a guide. *Note: Be sure to cut on a proper surface.*

Transfer the appliqué, snap, and strap locations from the pattern onto the fabric and vinyl with a marking pen.

Cut the appliqué material in half and cement the pieces with the wrong sides together, making a 6" x 6" (15.2 x 15.2 cm) square. Cut out the appliqué circle according to the pattern. Paint the edge of the appliqué circle with matching acrylic paint.

Cut the webbing into two pieces, one measuring 46" (116.8 cm) and the other 12" (30.5 cm).

Instructions

01

Stitch half of the magnetic snap set behind the flap lining and the other half behind the outside front as marked on the pattern.

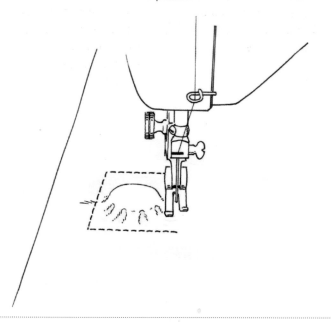

02

Clip the outside flap and flap lining together with the right sides together. Stitch around the flap using a ⅜" (1 cm) seam allowance. Leave 6" (15.2 cm) open along the back edge to turn the flap right side out in step 3.

03

Turn the flap right side out through the hole along the back edge. Topstitch all around the flap ⅛" (3 mm) away from the edge.

04

Adhere the appliqué piece to the flap with cement or double-sided tape as noted on the pattern. Stitch around the appliqué, through the flap, ⅛" (3 mm) from the edge.

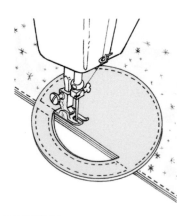

05

Sew the D-rings onto the end of the long piece of webbing. Fold ⅜" (1 cm) under and stitch as close to the D-rings as possible using a zipper foot. Cover the tip of the 12" (30.5 cm) piece of webbing with the tab of vinyl.

06

Sew the ends of the webbing onto the gussets, folding ¾" (1.9 cm) under and stitching a box stitch as marked on the pattern.

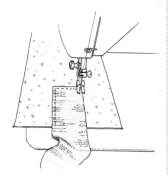

07

Topstitch the flap onto the back section of the bag as marked on the pattern.

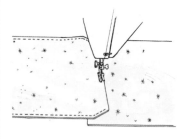

08

Clip the gussets in place to either side of the front/bottom/back piece, making sure to match up the notches. Stitch using a ⅜" (1 cm) seam allowance.

09

Fold the short ends of the lining pocket piece ¼" (6 mm) and ¼" (6 mm) again using pins or double-sided tape. Topstitch ⅛" (3 mm) away from the edge.

10

Pin the lining pocket to the front/bottom/back lining piece. Topstitch across the bottom lines and down the center front as marked on the patterns.

11

Pin the lining gussets to the lining front/bottom/back piece, making sure to match up the notches. Stitch using a ⅜" (1 cm) seam allowance.

12

Drop the assembled lining into the assembled outside with the right sides together. Clip together and stitch around the top edge using a ⅜" (1 cm) seam allowance. Leave a 6" (15.2 cm) opening along the back section to turn the bag right side out in step 13.

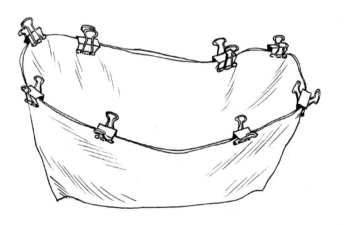

13

Turn the bag right side out through the opening along the back section. Clip and topstitch around the top edge ⅛" (3 mm) away from the edge.

14

Machine or hand tack the top of all four corners of the gussets to create a neat finish.

Kauai Tote

Surf's up on our keyhole-handled tote. This silhouette is the perfect fashion accessory for a picnic lunch on the beach or coffee with friends around the pool. The Kauai tote features an inside wall pocket made from a coated cotton palm tree print and sports a clear vinyl handle. Hang ten with a style of your own. Try using different lining fabric for a contrasting look or add more pockets and hang them on the outside. Either way, the Kauai tote is sure to catch the perfect stylish "wave" anytime!

Getting Started

Trace the Kauai tote bag patterns with a marking pen and cut out the fabric pieces with scissors. Trace and cut the vinyl with scissors or use a weight or loops of tape to hold down the patterns and cut with a knife.

Line up the metal ruler along the straight edges of the patterns while cutting out the vinyl pieces with a utility knife. When cutting rounded edges, simply use the edge of your pattern as a guide. *Note: Be sure to cut on a proper surface.*

Transfer the hole locations from the pattern onto the fabric and vinyl with a marking pen.

MATERIALS

36" x 36" (91.5 x 91.5 cm) piece of vinyl-coated cotton

8" x 18" (20.5 x 46 cm) piece of ⅛" (3 mm) -thick clear vinyl

16 sets of ¼" (6 mm) screw posts

matching thread for machine sewing

TOOLS

rotary or handheld hole punch, size #9 (¼" [6 mm])

cardboard, 8-oz. leather, or wood for punching board (if using handheld punch)

utility knife

12" (30.5 cm) and 24" (61 cm) metal rulers

masking tape and/or pattern weights

rawhide mallet or hammer

binder clips

marking pen

flat-head screw driver

scissors

patterns (see page 93)

MACHINERY

home sewing machine with a Teflon foot

Instructions

01

Use binder clips to clip the outside pieces with the right sides together. Stitch across the bottom using a ⅜" (1 cm) seam allowance. Back tack at the beginning and end of the seam.

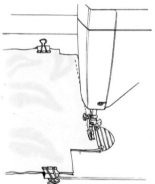

02

Topstitch ⅛" (3 mm) on both sides of the bottom seam on the right side of the fabric.

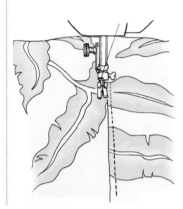

03

Use binder clips to clip the outside pieces with the right sides together. Stitch along the sides using a ⅜" (1 cm) seam allowance. Back tack at the beginning and end of the seam.

04

Topstitch ⅛" (3 mm) on both sides of the side seams on the right side of the fabric.

05

With the right sides together, match the side and bottom seams and then stitch straight across the opening using a ⅜" (1 cm) seam allowance. The bottom seam should be perpendicular to the side seams.

06

With the right sides together, sew the lining pieces together, stitching down the sides using a ⅜" (1 cm) seam allowance. Top stitch ⅛" (3 mm) on both sides of the side seams on the right side of the fabric. Stitch across the bottom, leaving a 6" (15 cm) opening for turning in step 8. Stitch the corners closed as in step 5.

07

Drop the lining into the outside of the bag so that the right sides of both fabrics are together. Clip together and stitch around the top edge using a ⅜" (1 cm) seam allowance.

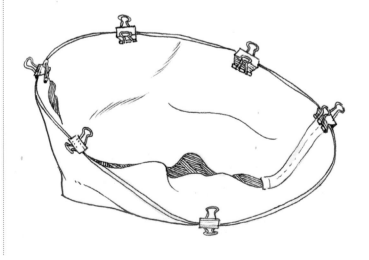

08

Turn the bag right-side out through the hole in the bottom of the lining. Topstitch the lining bottom closed.

09

Topstitch two rows of stitches around the top of the bag. The first row is ⅛" (3 mm) from the top edge of the bag, and the second row is ⅝" (1.6 cm) from the top edge.

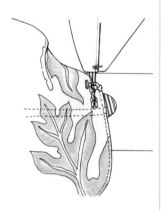

10

Sew around the two front pocket pieces with the right sides together using a ⅜" (1 cm) seam allowance. Leave a 4" (10 cm) opening at the bottom edge. Clip the excess fabric off the corners and turn right side out.

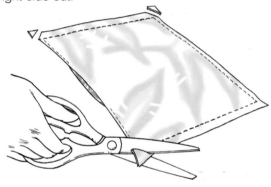

11

Repeat the previous step to make the two back pocket pieces.

12

Topstitch ⅛" (3 mm) from the edge across the top of the front pocket piece. Clip the front pocket piece to the back pocket piece, lining up the bottom edges. Topstitch ⅛" (3 mm) from the edge all around the pocket. Back tack at the top corners of front pocket piece to add strength.

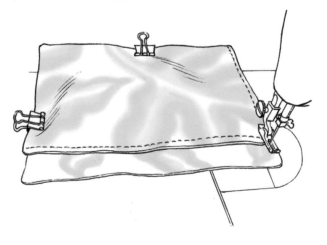

13

Punch ¼" (6 mm) holes in vinyl pieces, pocket, and through the sewn bag as labeled on the patterns. Remember to use a punching board to protect work surfaces.

14

Attach vinyl handles onto the bag with ¼" (6 mm) screw posts using a flat-head screw driver. Line up the pocket with the center back four holes. Overlap the front piece of vinyl onto the back piece at the side seams.

Nine-to-Five Messenger Bag

If it's sophistication, class, and attitude you want, check out our stylish messenger bag. Made of simulated leather-look vinyl, it features an adjustable shoulder strap and inside organizer pockets. Sporting an additional briefcase top handle, this durable solution to the nine-to-five crunch will carry you through even the toughest of days in style.

Getting Started

Trace the messenger bag patterns with a marking pen and cut out all vinyl, fabric, interfacing, and craft foam pieces with scissors or use a weight or loops of tape to hold down the patterns and cut with a knife.

Line up the metal ruler along the straight edges of the patterns while cutting out the vinyl pieces with a utility knife. When cutting rounded edges, simply use the edge of your pattern as a guide. *Note: Be sure to cut on a proper surface.*

Transfer the zipper, tuck catch lock, strap, and rivet locations from the pattern onto the vinyl with a marking pen. *Note: Tuck catch locks vary in size, so be sure to mark the prong slots to match your lock.*

Cut two strips of outside fabric for the piping to each measure 30" x 1¼" (76.2 x 3.2 cm). Cement the strips in half, with the piping filler in the center, matching raws edges of the vinyl (see illustration below). Use bone folder to sandwich the cording into place.

Cut the 60" (152.4 cm) piece of webbing into two pieces, one measuring 50" (127 cm) and the other 10" (25.4 cm).

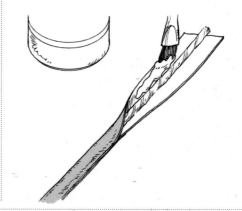

MATERIALS

36" x 36" (91.4 x 91.4 cm) piece of vinyl fabric

36" x 36" (91.4 x 91.4 cm) piece of vinyl-coated cotton lining fabric

36" x 36" (91.4 x 91.4 cm) piece of medium-weight interfacing

30" x 1¼" (76.2 x 3.2 cm) vinyl fabric

1" x 2" (2.5 x 5.1 cm) brass tuck catch lock

1½" (3.8 cm) brass strap loop

1½" (3.8 cm) brass strap single bar slide

60" (152.4 cm) piece of 1½" (3.8 cm) webbing for strap

10" (25.4 cm) piece of 1¼" (3.2 cm) webbing for handle

four 5/16" (8 mm) brass double-capped rivets

12" (30.5 cm) zipper

60" (152.4 cm) length of ⅛" (3 mm) cording for piping filler

5" x 14" (12.7 x 35.6 cm) piece of craft foam

matching thread for machine sewing

TOOLS

rotary or handheld hole punch, size 2 (⅛" [3 mm])

cardboard, 8 oz. leather, or wood for punching board (if using handheld hole punch)

rivet-setting kit

utility or craft knife

needle-nose pliers

12" (30.5 cm) and 24" (61 cm) metal rulers

masking tape and/or pattern weights

rubber cement or fabric glue

double-sided craft tape (¼" [6 mm] wide)

binder clips

marking pen

scissors

straight pins

patterns (see page 105)

MACHINERY

home sewing machine with a Teflon foot and zipper foot

Instructions

01

Clip the outside flap, flap interfacing, and flap lining pieces together with the right sides of the vinyl together. Stitch around the flap using a ⅜" (1 cm) seam allowance. Leave 6" (15.2 cm) open along the back edge to turn the flap right side out in step 2.

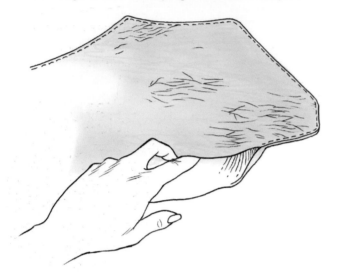

02

Turn the flap right side out through the hole along the back edge. Topstitch all around the flap ⅛" (3 mm) away from the edge.

03

Topstitch the 1¼" (3.2 cm) webbing handle to the top of the flap folding ¾" (1.9 cm) under as marked on the pattern.

04

Set the tuck catch lock tab onto the flap, using a utility knife to make small slits for the hardware. Push the hardware through the front of the tab and fold the ends down with needle-nose pliers.

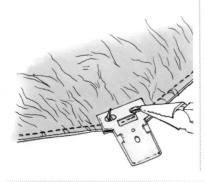

05

Use a utility knife to cut small slits through the outside front and interfacing to set the other half of the tuck catch lock as marked on the pattern. Stick the prongs through the fabric and bend them over the washer on the back side.

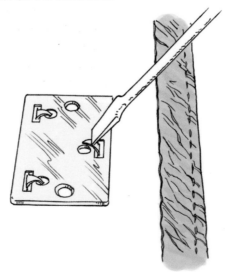

06

Cut out the window for the zipper on the front section of the interfacing. Clip, pin, or use double-sided tape to hold the interfacing to the outside front piece.

07

Slice the opening for the zipper pocket in the outside front as marked on the pattern. Fold the allowance of the outside fabric over the interfacing using cement or double-sided tape. Cement or tape the zipper into position in the center of the window. Fold one end of the pocket piece and line it up underneath the right-hand side on the zipper.

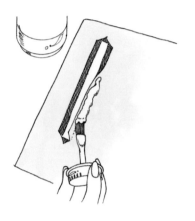

08

Topstitch along the right-hand side of the zipper, catching the pocket fabric underneath.

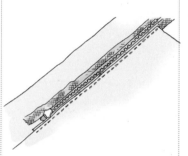

09

Fold the pocket fabric under the zipper and line up along the left-hand side of the zipper. Topstitch around the other three sides of the zipper, catching the pocket fabric underneath.

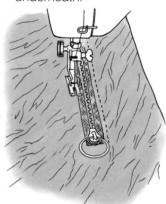

10

Pull the outside front piece out of the way and stitch the sides of the pocket fabric closed using a ⅜" (1 cm) seam allowance.

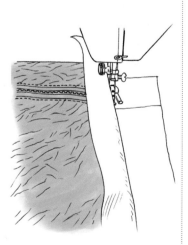

11

Sew the outside front piece to the outside bottom piece using a ⅜" (1 cm) seam allowance.

12

Clip, pin, or use double-sided tape to hold the interfacing back piece to the wrong side of the outside back piece. Sew the outside back piece to the outside bottom piece using a ⅜" (1 cm) seam allowance.

13

Use cement or double-sided tape to secure the craft foam piece in the center of the wrong side of the bottom.

Instructions

14

Topstitch the flap onto the back section of the bag as marked on the pattern.

15

Sew the piping around the edge of each gusset using a zipper foot and a ⅜" (1 cm) seam allowance. Clip into the seam allowance of the piping where it turns the corner of the gusset for a smooth fit. Taper the piping out into the seam allowance ¾" (1.9 cm) below the top edge.

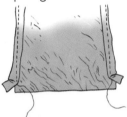

16

Stay stitch the 50" (127 cm) webbing strap into place in the seam allowance on the back edge of one gusset as marked on the pattern. Fold the 10" (25.4 cm) piece of webbing through the strap loop and stitch it into place in the seam allowance on the back edge of the other gusset as marked on the pattern. Extend the ends of the webbing an extra 1" (2.5 cm) beyond the seam allowance to be riveted in step 25.

17

Clip the gussets in place to both sides of the front/bottom/back piece, making sure to match up the notches and the strap coming out of the back edge. Stitch using a ⅜" (1 cm) seam allowance.

18

Fold the top edges of the lining pocket pieces ¼" (6 mm) and ¼" (6 mm) again using pins or double-sided tape. Topstitch ⅛" (3 mm) away from the edge.

19

Clip or pin one lining pocket to the front lining piece. Stay stitch down the side edges ¼" (6 cm) away from the edge. Topstitch down the center of the front pocket as marked on the patterns.

20

Clip or pin the other lining pocket to the back lining piece. Stay stitch down the side edges ¼" (6 cm) away from the edge.

21

Sew the front and back lining pieces to the bottom lining piece using a ⅜" (1 cm) seam allowance. Topstitch across the bottom seams ⅛" (3 mm) away from the edge.

22

Pin the lining gussets in place to either side of the front/bottom/back lining piece, making sure to match up the notches. Stitch using a ⅜" (1 cm) seam allowance.

23

Use a size #2 (⅛" [3 mm]) rotary or handheld hole punch to punch through the gusset and the strap webbing as marked on the pattern. Make sure to use a punching board underneath the gusset.

24

Set all ⁵⁄₁₆" (8 mm) double-capped rivets through the gusset fabric, interfacing, and webbing with a rivet-setting kit.

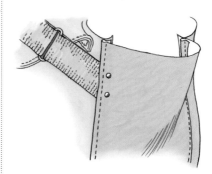

25

Thread the 50" (127 cm) piece of webbing through the single bar slide, then through the strap loop and back around the center bar of the slide. Fold over the end and stitch the webbing to itself.

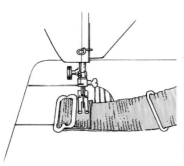

26

Drop the assembled lining into the assembled outside with the right sides together. Clip together and stitch around the top edge using a ⅜" (1 cm) seam allowance. Leave a 6" (15.2 cm) opening along the back section to turn the bag right side out in step 27.

27

Turn the bag right side out through the opening along the back section. Clip and topstitch around the top edge ⅛" (3 mm) away from the edge.

28

Machine or hand tack the top of all four corners of the gussets to create a neat finish.

The 8:08 Express Hobo Bag

When you think of a hobo-shaped bag, you expect to see a soft, unconstructed bag with a rounded top zipper and a single handle. The hobo shape was originally designed to emulate the sack carried by homeless men as they moved from town to town riding the rails. The hobo shape has become an all-time favorite of women of all ages, both as a staple and functional bag, as well as an evening bag. If you want at least one versatile and elegant hobo bag in your closet, our two-tone faux snakeskin and faux leather hobo is a great choice. Use your imagination and change the colors, textures, and ornamentations to create your own train stopper! Make the strap longer or enlarge the patterns to create a comfortable travel bag sure to stop the other commuters in their tracks.

Getting Started

Trace the hobo bag patterns with a marking pen or pencil and cut out from the vinyl, Pellon, and interfacing all pieces of the bag according to the patterns. (If vinyl is a substantial weight, you may omit the Pellon.) Use a weight or loops of masking tape to hold the patterns in place. Also cut out two 1½" x 1¼" (3.8 x 3.2 cm) strips of vinyl for the ends of the zipper.

Note: Test a sample of the fusible interfacing first to make sure it is compatible with your vinyl when ironed; otherwise, use rubber cement or craft glue.

MATERIALS

1 yard (91.4 cm) lightweight to medium-weight faux-leather vinyl (for outside panels, tabs, handle lining, and interior lining)

½ yard (45.7 cm) lightweight to medium-weight snakeskin-embossed vinyl (for outside panels and outside handle)

30" x 24" (76.2 x 61 cm) piece of lightweight to medium-weight Pellon interfacing or craft felt (optional)

5" x 7" (12.7 x 17.8 cm) piece of medium-weight fusible interfacing

two 1¼" (3.2 cm) O-rings

17" (43.2 cm) zipper

eight ¼" (6 mm)-long rivets

thread for machine sewing

spray adhesive *Note: Test first.*

rubber cement or craft glue

TOOLS

rotary or handheld hole punch, size #2 (⅛" [3 mm])

rivet-setting kit

iron

bone folder

hand sewing needle

scissors

masking tape and/or pattern weights

rawhide mallet or hammer

silver pen or fabric marking pen/pencil

binder clips

patterns (see page 98)

MACHINERY

home sewing machine with a Teflon foot and 1/8" (3 mm) topstitch foot

Instructions

01

Using spray adhesive (or rubber cement or craft glue), attach the Pellon pieces to the wrong side of each corresponding vinyl piece within the seam allowance.

02

Using binder clips, attach the five panels for the front and the five panels for the back to their corresponding seams, good sides facing each other. Sew from top to bottom of each seam using a Teflon foot at ⅜" (1 cm), back tacking at the beginning and end of the stitch line.

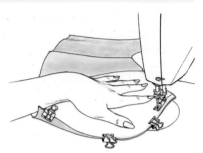

Using rubber cement or craft glue, press the seams open. Topstitch ⅛" (3 mm) along either side of each seam.

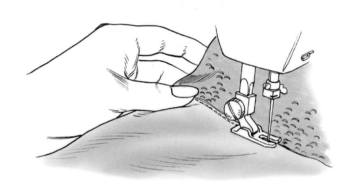

03

Using binder clips, clip the darts of the lining together, good sides facing each other, and stitch all darts at a ⅜" (1 cm) seam allowance, using the Teflon foot.

04

Using binder clips, clip the short ends of each precut ½" x 1¼" (1.3 x 3.2 cm) strip of vinyl to the ends of the zipper, good sides facing good side of zipper. Sew across short ends at a ⅜" (1 cm) seam allowance with a Teflon foot. Pull the strips open and topstitch at ⅛" (3 mm) on vinyl using the topstitch foot.

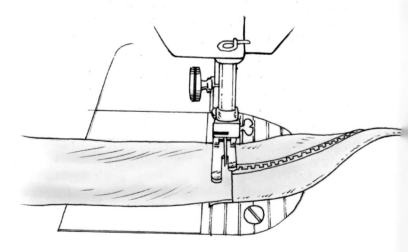

05

Using binder clips, clip and sew the zipper between the outside vinyl and lining using a ⅜" (1 cm) seam allowance, back tacking at the beginning and end of the stitch line. Be sure the right side of the zipper is facing the right side of the vinyl. Repeat for the other side of the zipper.

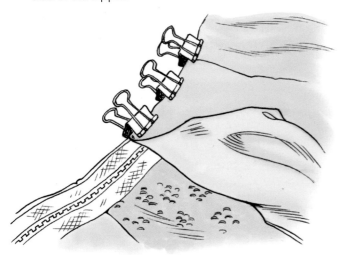

06

Topstitch the seam on either side of the zipper ⅛" (3 mm) away from the edge using a gauge foot.

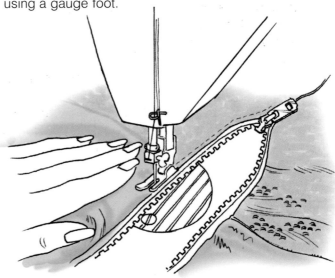

07

Clip together all around the sides and bottom of the outside front and back pieces, good sides facing each other. Using the Teflon foot, stitch all around the sides and the bottom on the ⅜" (1 cm) seam allowance line, back tacking at the beginning and end of the stitch line. Be sure to unzip the zipper before sewing! Clip and partially stitch the lining together at the ⅜" (1 cm) seam allowance, leaving a 6" (15.2 cm) opening in the center bottom to turn the bag right side out.

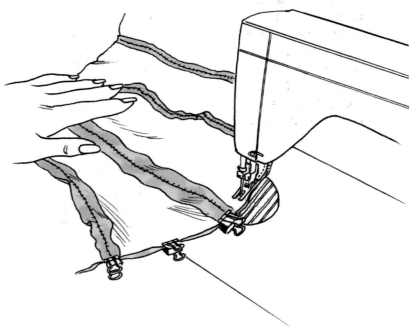

Instructions

08

Turn the bag right side out through the opening in the bottom seam of the lining. Fold, clip, and top-stitch the opening of the lining closed.

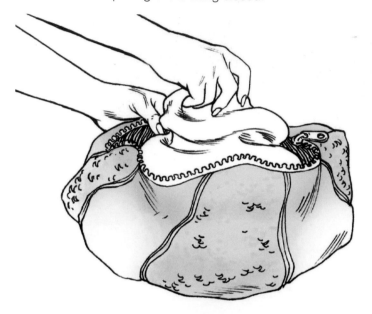

09

Iron the precut fusible interfacing tab pieces to the wrong side of the vinyl tabs. Using rubber cement or craft glue, glue and turn the vinyl edges around the edge of fusible interfacing using a bone folder. Pleat the vinyl around the rounded ends of the fusible tabs and clip away any excess with scissors. Mark the tabs for rivet placement with a marking pen. Topstitch all around the tabs ⅛" (3 mm) away from the edge using a gauge foot.

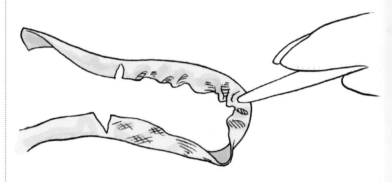

10

Fold the tabs over the O-rings and hand tack on either side of the tab directly under the O-ring to secure it in place. Secure two tabs to each O-ring (one to attach to the handle, the other to attach to the bag). Punch holes for the rivets in the tabs with a hole punch.

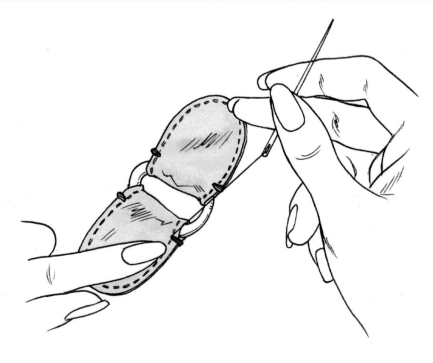

11

Sew down the long ends of the handle, good sides facing each other, at a ⅜" (1 cm) seam allowance. Turn the handle right side out through the short end. Make a box pleat on either end of the handle and stitch closed. Insert the ends of the handle between the tabs. Punch holes through the handles with a hole punch using the holes in the tabs as your guide. Using a rivet-setting kit, secure the tabs to the handle.

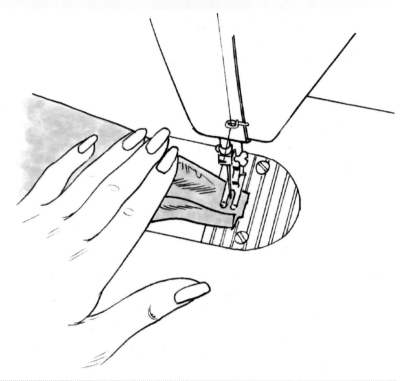

12

Insert the top corners of the bag between the remaining tabs. Punch holes through the bag using the holes in the tabs as your guide.

Using a rivet-setting kit, secure the tabs to the bag.

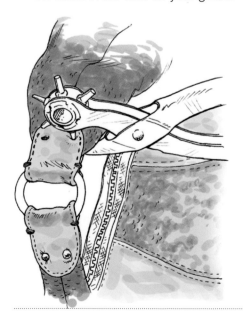

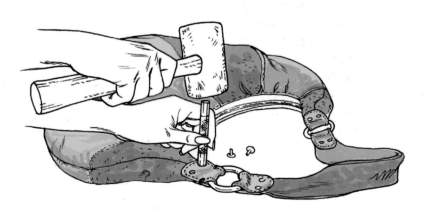

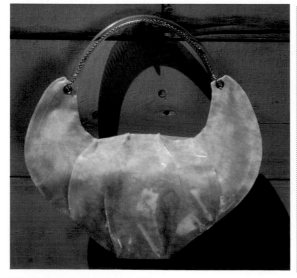

Indianapolis Speedway Hobo Bag

Do you have any rubber tires hanging around taking up space in your garage? Here's our recycling solution: turn that inner tube into a contemporary, high functioning "Indianapolis Speedway" hobo bag. Sporting rubber tubing handles, grommets, and lacing with metal nut and washer accents, this bag has the sleek lines of a classic with the chassis of a hot rod. For variations, try contrasting lacing or replace the metal findings with wood or plastic beads. You can also eliminate the hanging fringe altogether, for a more stream-lined look, or change the materials entirely to keep a clean, bright silhouette.

Getting Started

Trace the hobo bag patterns onto the inner tube with the marking pen. Arrange them as you like, but be sure to place the end pattern pieces so that the outer edge falls on the outer edge of the tube (as noted on the pattern).

Use pattern weights or loops of masking tape to hold the patterns in place while tracing. Be sure to transfer all markings for the hole punches. Cut out with scissors. Use binder clips to hold the end pieces together, because you will be cutting them out two layers at a time.

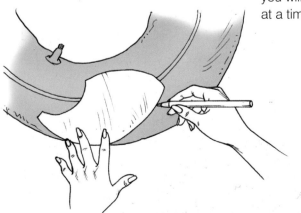

MATERIALS

standard auto tire inner tube

30' of ⅛" (3 mm) neoprene cording (other cording may be substituted)

ten ½" (1.3 cm) grommets

two 45" (114.3 cm) lengths of ½" (1.3 cm) rubber cording

two ½" (1.3 cm)-long rivets

approximately thirty-five ¼" (6 mm) hardware nuts and sixteen ¼" (6 mm) washers (for trim on hanging cording)

slider to fit ⅛" (3 mm) cording

TOOLS

rotary or handheld hold punch, size #2 (⅛" [3 mm])

cardboard, 8 oz. leather, or wood for punching board

rivet-setting kit

½" (1.3 cm) handheld punch

grommet-setting kit

scissors

masking tape and/or pattern weights

rawhide mallet or hammer

gel roller marking pen

awl

needle-nose pliers

binder clips

patterns (see page 96)

Instructions

01

Punch out the lacing holes with the rotary or size #2 handheld hole punch.

Punch ½" (1.3 cm) holes for the grommets with the ½" (1.3 cm) handheld punch. Set the grommets with the grommet-setting kit.

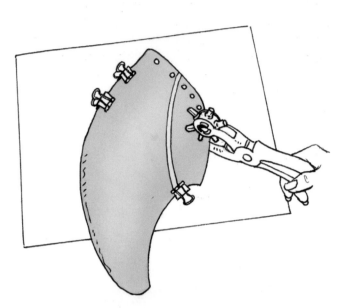

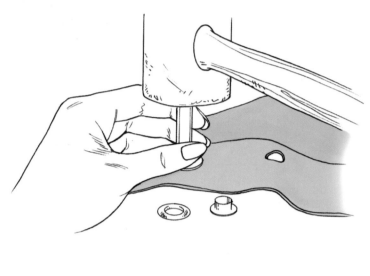

02

Cut four pieces from the ⅛" (3 mm) cording into 38" (96.5 cm) lengths. Make a knot in the cord, leaving a tail, and start on the bottom outer corner of panels labeled "2 left and right" on the pattern. Start whip stitching the panels labeled "2 left and right" to the end pieces, starting at the bottom and working your way up.

When you get to the top corners, stitch through the top corner holes twice, then continue around the top edge of panel 2, stitching through the next set of corner holes twice also. Attach the center panel by continuing to whip stitch down until you get to the bottom. Tie a knot in the cord, leaving a tail. Repeat for the three other sections. *Note: Be sure not to get the panel seam holes confused with the side/bottom holes.*

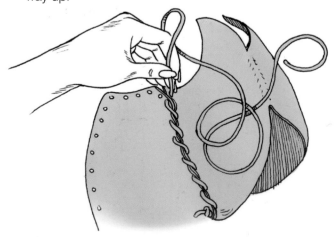

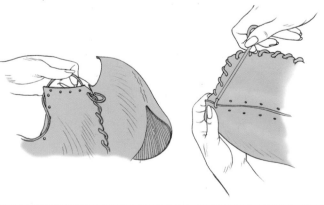

03

Cut two pieces from the ⅛" (3 mm) cording into 33" (83.8 cm) lengths. Make a knot in the cord, leaving a tail, and start whip stitching the sides and bottom (front and back) together, beginning at the first hole under the fold on the side panels. Stop when you get to the last hole before the center. Tie a knot in the cord, leaving a tail. Repeat for the other half. Now cut two pieces of the ⅛" (3 mm) cord into 19" (48.3 cm) lengths. Whip stitch the top corners of the sides together. Leave a tail at the top, knot it, whip stitch to the last hole before the fold, tie a knot, and leave a tail.

At this point you may tie the tails hanging along the bottom from panels "2 left and right," securing two cords together, so that they hang down straight. String on some of the nuts and washers to the ends of the tails and tie off.

04

To attach the handle, trim ends of the ½" (1.3 cm) rubber cording at sharp angles. Start at the center of the front half and weave in and out through the grommets, coming out from behind the top outer corners back and forth until both ends come out in front center. Join the angled ends of the cut handle so that they are flush with each other and punch two holes through both layers; set rivets through them, making sure the handle is securely joined.

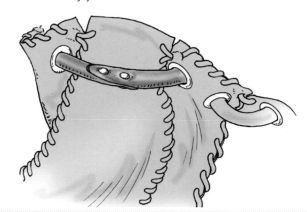

05

Cut the remaining ⅛" (3 mm) cording in half. Loop one of the pieces around the joined handle seam, over and over until the rivets are hidden. Leave tails at the end, securing by passing each end underneath the loops to the other side with the needle-nose pliers, and tie in a knot.

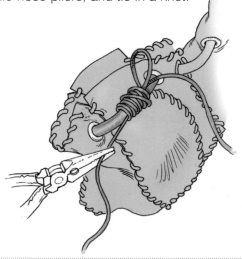

String on the nuts and washers, and tie off. Repeat for the back half of the bag, this time instead of leaving hanging tails in the back, lace the cords through the top holes in the center section, making the top edge fold in; tie in a knot. Continue the two cords through to the front half through the top center holes in the same fashion. When the cords are through the front, attach a slider to keep the bag closed. String the nuts and washers and tie off.

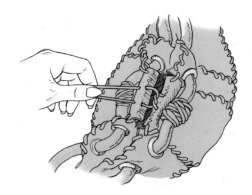

Jamba Gym Bag

Hit the gym in style this year with our multicolored vinyl gym bag, which is just the right size to fit your shoes, a change of clothes, and your favorite after-workout beverage. The lining is waterproof so there's no need to worry about stains. This unisex bag takes anyone to the gym in style. Change the color scheme to match your outerwear, favorite palette, or mood. Remember, this would also be a great gift for Dad!

MATERIALS

30" x 21" (76.2 x 53.3 cm) piece of upholstery vinyl (gray)

40" x 20" (101.6 x 50.8 cm) piece of upholstery vinyl (orange)

30" x 21" (76.2 x 53.3 cm) piece of upholstery vinyl (blue)

39" x 29" (99.1 x 73.7 cm) piece of medium-weight lightweight vinyl for lining

10" x 1½" (25.4 x 3.8 cm) strip of thin, flexible vinyl for pocket binding

two lengths of 40" (101.6 cm)-long premade piping (or two strips 40" x 1¼" [101.6 x 3.2 cm], and two tabs measuring 1½" x 1" [3.8 x 2.5 cm] from thin, flexible vinyl, and two 40" [101.6 cm] pieces of ³⁄₁₆" [4.8 mm] cording for piping)

48" (121.9 cm) length of wide bias tape (to bind edges of lining)

two pieces of 23" (58.4 cm) x ½" (1.3 cm) flexible cording or tubing (for handles)

four ½" (1.3 cm)-long rivets

twelve ⅜" (1 cm)-long rivets

22" (55.9 cm) zipper

four 1" (2.5 cm) D-rings

six hardware feet for bottom of bag (long-pronged studs may be substituted)

edge dye/acrylic paint (with applicator paintbrush or dauber)

approximately 36" (91.4 cm) of thin- or medium-gauge wire (to feed tubing through handle)

thread for machine sewing

TOOLS

rotary or handheld hole punch, #2 (⅛" [3 mm])

cardboard, 8 oz. leather, or wood for punching board (if using handheld punch)

utility knife

12" (30.5 cm) and 24" (61 cm) metal rulers

cutting mat

rivet-setting kit

bone folder

binder clips

scissors

¼" double-sided craft tape

¼" (6 mm) wide masking tape and/or pattern weights

rawhide mallet or hammer

gel roller marking pen

awl

needle-nose pliers

rubber cement or craft/latex glue

patterns (see page 114)

MACHINERY

home sewing machine with a Teflon foot, ⅛" (3 mm) gauge foot, and zipper foot

Getting Started

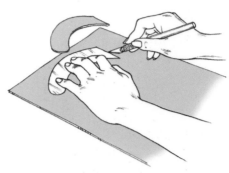

When cutting all pieces for this project, use pattern weights or loops of tape to hold down the pattern and cut the vinyl with a utility knife. Line up the metal ruler along the straight edges of the patterns while cutting out the vinyl pieces with a utility knife. When cutting rounded edges, simply use the edge of your pattern as a guide. *Note: Be sure to cut on a proper surface.*

Cut out an 11" x 11" (27.9 x 27.9 cm) piece of both the orange and blue vinyl. Cement or glue together, good sides facing outward, and cut the side pocket flap and D-ring tabs from the patterns out of this piece. Note: Be sure to cut two of the tabs with the pattern flipped over. Cut out a 21" x 15" (53.3 x 38.1 cm) piece of both the gray and blue vinyl. Cement or glue together, good sides facing outward, and cut the front pocket and corner pieces from the pattern out of this piece. *Note: Be sure to cut two of the corners with the pattern flipped over.*

Cut out a 9" x 6" (22.9 x 15.2 cm) piece of both the orange and gray vinyl. Cement or glue together, good sides facing outward, and cut the side pocket from the pattern out of this piece. Cut the remaining vinyl pieces as labeled on the patterns.

Transfer the locations for the hardware feet onto the bottom piece and rivet placement onto the handle piece with a marking pen or awl. Transfer and punch the holes for the rivets through the D-ring tabs and front/back pieces. Using acrylic paint or edge dye, paint the rounded edges of the corner and all around the D-ring tab pieces.

To make the piping, cement or glue both pieces of the cording down the centers of the 1¼" x 40" (3.2 x 101.6 cm) pieces of thin vinyl. Fold the vinyl over the cording, matching up the raw edges of the vinyl. Use a bone folder to sandwich the cording into place. Use scissors to clip every ⅛" (3 mm) along the seam allowance of the piping. Note: Do not clip all the way to cording, or it will show in the finished bag.

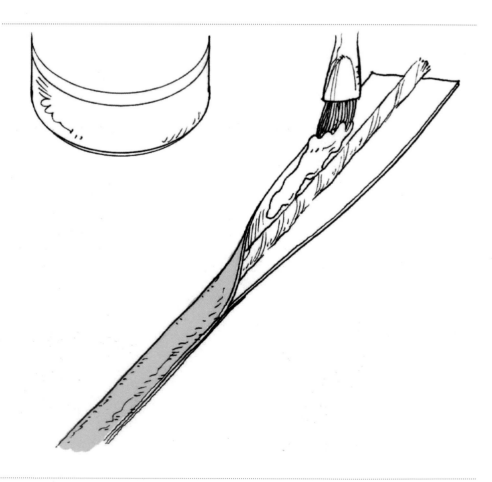

Instructions

01

Using double-sided tape, attach the bottom vinyl reinforcement onto the back of the outside bottom piece, making sure to keep it centered. Insert the feet into the bottom piece by poking an awl through the bottom piece (and reinforcement), inserting the feet, and bending the prongs open (or by cutting slits with a knife and prying the prongs open, depending on the type of feet used). Place pieces of masking tape over the opened prongs. Cement or glue the bottom lining to the inside (reinforcement side) of the bottom piece

02

Using the ⅛" (3 mm) gauge foot, topstitch the following: all around the outer edge of bottom, attaching the lining piece; along the top edge of the side pocket; all around the D-ring tabs; and all around the flap edge of the side pocket flap (straight up to the top edge of the flap, sewing over the small side tabs sticking out from the sides). Place the side pocket on top of a side gusset piece using double-sided tape around the edges, matching up the bottom and side edges of both pieces. Attach the pocket to the gusset by stitching all around sides and bottom with the gauge foot.

03

Using binder clips, clip and sew the zipper between the outside vinyl and lining top-zip pieces using a ⅜" (1 cm) seam allowance, back tacking at the beginning and end of the stitch line. Be sure the right side of the zipper is facing the right side of the vinyl. Repeat for the other side of the zipper. Pull back the top-zip outside and lining pieces tightly, so that the zipper is exposed. Topstitch the seam on either side of the zipper ⅛" (3 mm) away from the edge using a gauge foot.

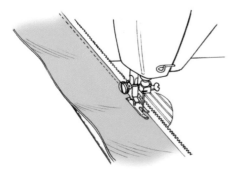

04

Using binder clips, clip and sew an end of the top-zip piece between an outside vinyl and lining gusset piece using a ⅜" (1 cm) seam allowance, back tacking at the beginning and end of the stitch line. Be sure the right side of the zipper is facing the right side of the outside gusset. Repeat for the other side with the other gusset (with the side pocket). Pull back the gusset pieces tightly and topstitch on the top edges of the gussets, ⅛" (3 mm) away from the seam, using a gauge foot. Cement or glue the outside gusset to the gusset lining.

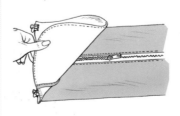

Place double-sided tape on the top edge of the side pocket flap on the gusset side with the pocket, lining up the top edge of the flap on the seam where the gusset and top-zip pieces are attached. Topstitch the top edge of the flap to the gusset, using the gauge foot.

Instructions

05

Cement or glue the front pocket lining to the inside of the front pocket. Make a "French-bound" edge on top of the pocket by clipping the 10" x 1½" (25.4 x 3.8 cm) strip of thin vinyl to the top edge of the pocket. Be sure the good side of the strip is facing the outside of the pocket, and the raw edges match up. Stitch the top edge of the pocket to the strip with the gauge foot. Cement or glue the inside of the strip to the top inside edge of the pocket, folding the strip over and around the top edge of the pocket, exposing the good side of the strip to look like piping. Using a zipper foot, "stitch-in-the-ditch" of the seam, directly under the seamed edge (on the good side of the pocket). Using scissors, trim the excess of the strip close to the stitched edge on the inside of the pocket.

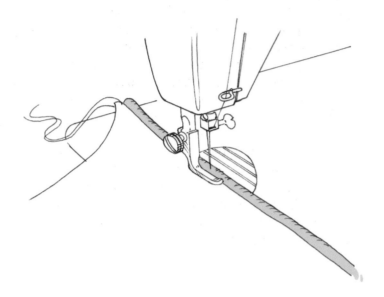

06

Place the D-ring tabs onto the front/back pieces as noted on the pattern. Using a rivet-setting kit, set ⅜" (1 cm) rivets through the bottom two holes of the tabs. Loop the tops of the tabs through the D-rings (from behind the D-ring over to the front) and set ⅜" (1 cm) rivets through the tabs, attaching the D-rings to the tabs and to the front/back pieces.

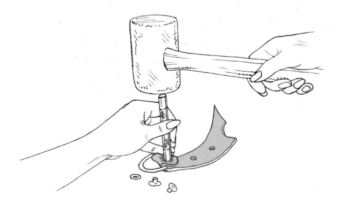

07

Using double-sided tape, attach the side and bottom edges of the front pocket to the front of the bag as noted on the pattern. Then, using double-sided tape, attach the curved edge of the corner pieces to the front and back pieces, as noted on the pattern. Topstitch around the curved edge of the corner pieces, using the gauge foot. This will attach both the corners and pocket to the front piece (and corners to the back piece). Cement or glue the front and back lining pieces to the inside of the outside front and back pieces.

08

Using binder clips, clip the long ends of the bottom pieces to the bottom edges of the front and back pieces, good sides facing each other. Stitch each side, one at a time, using a ⅜" (1 cm) seam allowance with a Teflon foot. Trim approximately ³⁄₁₆" (4.8 mm) off the seam allowance with scissors. Cut off two pieces of the bias tape long enough for the length of each seam. Center the bias tape (lengthwise) on the edge of the seam and fold it around both sides, encasing the seam in between it. Hold in place with the double-sided tape and/or binder clips. Sew in place all along the length of the bias tape with a Teflon foot, creating a bound edge. Try to sew on the same stitch line as sewn previously when the bottom was attached to the front and back pieces.

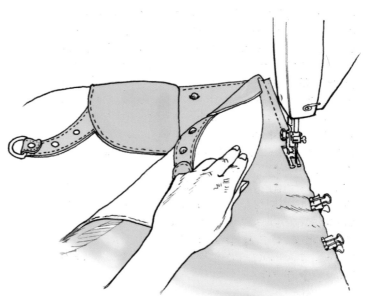

09

To sew the piping to the bag, center one of the pre-cut 1¼" x 1" (3.2 x 2.5 cm) tabs on one of the bottom side's edges at the notch, good side to good side, placing the 1" (2.5 cm) raw edge of the tab to the edge of the bottom. Using binder clips, clip the piping all around the front half of the bag, raw edge to raw edge, until you get to the center of the bottom on the other side.

Begin sewing the piping to the vinyl, centering the piping on top of the tab. Use a zipper foot to sew the piping all around the bag, until you almost reach the center of the bottom on the other side. Cut the piping so that the end is centered directly above the center notch of the bottom piece. Place the other tab, centered in the same fashion as previously described, underneath the end of the cord. Place the end of the other piece of piping so that it butts up to the first piece, fold the tab over the piping ends, and stitch the tab down. Clip the second piece of piping all around the back half of the bag and sew all around. When you get to the starting point, cut the piping so that it butts up to the beginning piece, fold the tab over the piping ends, and stitch the tab down.

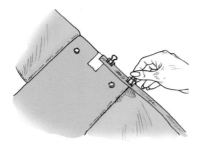
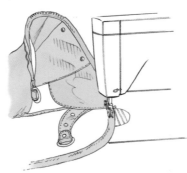

Instructions

10

Using binder clips, clip the top-zip/gusset piece to the front/bottom/back piece all around, good sides facing each other, being sure to match up at all center notches. Make sure you leave the zipper open. Using the zipper foot, sew all around at a ⅜" (1 cm) seam allowance; this should be on the same stitch line as the piping. Trim the seam allowance, attach the bias tape, and stitch all around as done in step 8. This time, however, start the bias tape at either the center front/back or center gusset, sew all around the entire bag until you get to the starting point, overlap 1" (2.5 cm), and cut an end off. Turn the bag right side out through the opened zipper.

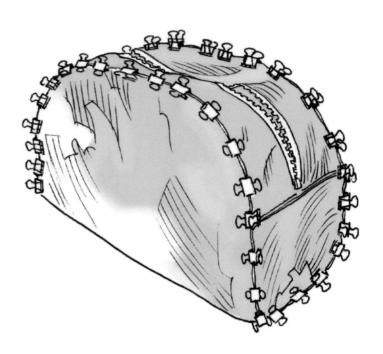

11

To make the handles, cement or glue the handle end pieces to the inside of the ends of the handles, being careful to match up the outer edges (good sides facing outward). Punch holes for rivets through the handle ends. Topstitch around the end parts only, using the gauge foot (outside of the handle facing you). Fold down the center of the main handle section lengthwise (good side facing outward), using binder clips to attach the raw edges together. Sew a channel down the length of the handle, wide enough to accommodate the ½" (1.3 cm) cording or tubing for the handle.

Note: Sew a test piece first from your vinyl to make sure that you allow enough room for the cording to pass through snugly, but not so snug that it is too difficult to pass through with ease.

Trim the excess from the edge of the handle seam with scissors, leaving about ⅛" (3 mm) from the stitch line. Using acrylic paint or edge dye, paint the raw edges of the handle all around.

12

Securely attach the wire around an end of one of the tubing/cording pieces by poking a hole or two through the tubing with the awl, threading the wire though it, and wrapping the wire around the tip several times. Feed the other end of the wire through the channel of the handle, and slowly pull the tubing through the channel using pliers until it comes out the other end. If the tubing stretched during this process, clip the ends of tubing off so that the tubing ends at the straight center section (not extending into the handle ends).

13

Loop one end of the handle through a D-ring on the front or back piece, feeding the end from the front of the D-ring to the back. Bring the side ends of the handle around, toward the front, sandwiching the inside of the handle between the outer side ends. Mark where rivet holes fall onto the side of the tubular handle, and punch hole through handle; line up all the rivet holes. Using a rivet-setting kit, set a ½" (1.3 cm) rivet through the end of the handle, securing the handle around the D-ring. Repeat for the other handle ends.

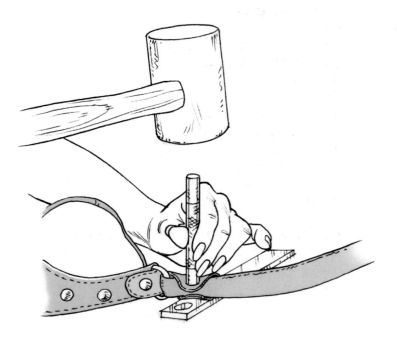

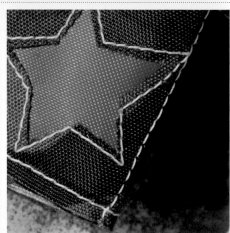

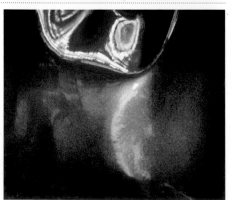

Section Three: Gallery

When it comes to accessories, the Fashion Institute of Technology (FIT) is probably the most creative school in the United States (and I'm not being biased!). When we took on the assignment of creating this book, it was with the idea of giving the patterns to our students to see what they would do with our designs. They were instructed to take the patterns and modify them, and encouraged to be as creative as they wanted. The following pages are the results of their creativity. Some students simply changed materials or modified the shape of the flap or length of the handle in the original pattern, whereas others went all out! Whatever they did, they brought our patterns and designs to a whole new level, creating pieces that are both fashion-forward and trendy.

Now it's your turn. Use their creations and ours as inspiration. Let your mind wander. Check out your drawers and closets for old tablecloths, showers mats and curtains, pieces of oil cloth, pieces of jewelry, or even parts of old handbags that are no longer useable. Salvage only those things that inspire you. Experiment with paint, colors, and sewing techniques that you would normally use on garments and home furnishings. Bring your creative personality to every accessory you make.

Remember: You are only as good and as creative as you want to be. Take your cue from our accessories design students, as they inspire great things for all of us.

Special thanks to the students from the Accessories Design Department of FIT for their interpretations of our patterns and for taking those designs over the top! They inspire us all!

TITLE: *Nicole*   **STUDENT:** Charles Christen   **PATTERN:** Diamond Plate Shopping Tote

Elegance doesn't have to cost a fortune, as exemplified by this sleek, bronze metallic vinyl bag. Accented with a simple gold clasp and licorice plastic look, our *Nicole* is perfect for lunching at the club or shopping at the mall.

TITLE: *Some Like It Hot*   **STUDENT:** Shara Cohn   **PATTERN:** Aloha Vanity Case

Why settle for an old and stodgy vanity case when you can add flair and color by creating your own one-of-a-kind?
This one screams pink in iridescent plastic accented with studs, knitted fruit, and an old necklace as a zipper pull.

TITLE: *Low Carb Gym Bag...Lightly Toasted* **STUDENT:** JoAnne Espinell **PATTERN:** Jamba Gym Bag

Low in fiber but very high in impact, this gym bag is made of coated printed cotton with contrasting solid vinyl patches and grommet accents. The bag also sports a rather impressive metal chain handle and contrasting zipper. Whether you're dieting or not, this bag will add just the right impact to any workout you've planned!

TITLE: *Pan Asian Sunset*   **STUDENT:** Angela Finochio   **PATTERN:** Retro Sparkle Messenger Bag

The messenger bag is one of the hottest silhouettes this season. Our "PA" sunset bag is made of natural coated cotton with an orange coated fabric appliquéd sunset on the flap. The body of the bag is a combination of neutral and orange coated cotton with a cotton webbed handle. Our bag sends just the right message to "orient" your timetable between work and play!

TITLE: *Guerilla Warfare* and *Guerilla*   **STUDENT:** Jennifer Hall   **PATTERN:** Holographic Techno-Wallet

Two wallets creating two distinctly different looks, one in camouflage coated fabric highlighted with inlay stars of red and the other made of red coated fabric highlighted with inlay stars of camouflage. Perfect for you and your favorite rebel.

TITLE: *Plastique*   **STUDENT:** Maria Napolitano   **PATTERN:** Diamond Plate Shopping Tote

A clear plastic shopping tote makes a wonderful and easy catchall for those hard-to-find items that tend to get lost in the bottom of your bag. Made of recycled clear plastic with contrasting stitching, this interpretation is a great project for children.

TITLE: *Joker Wallet*   **STUDENT:** Stefani Oblak   **PATTERN:** Holographic Techno-Wallet

Whether you've got a royal flush or a full house, this wallet is perfect for your poker nights and days. Made of pink clear plastic with playing-card inserts, our joker wallet is definitely "wild"!

TITLE: *Disco Crime Scene* **STUDENT:** Jessica Hymowitz **PATTERN:** Diamond Plate Shopping Tote

The evidence is clearly marked in this black and white checkerboard vinyl tote where colorful silkscreened handprints abound. There's no mystery to the multiple uses for this tote. Case closed!

TITLE: *Sunrise*   **STUDENT:** Shelley Parker   **PATTERN:** Retro Sparkle Messenger Bag

Sunrise or sunset, this messenger bag is anything but dull. Made of red woven fabric with yellow topstitching and yellow nylon web handles and closure, this bag showcases all the right bells and whistles.

TITLE: *Mellow Yellow* **STUDENT:** Shelley Parker **PATTERN:** Jamba Gym Bag

Miniature in size but not in impact, this mellow yellow coated cotton fabric bag with red webbed handles, coordinated zipper, red embossed plastic bottom, and topstitch accents is sure to bring back memories of school lockers, cafeterias, and being one of the "in" crowd.

TITLE: *Rush Hour Hobo*   **STUDENT:** Elise Pereira   **PATTERN:** The 8:08 Express Hobo Bag

Whether rushing to catch a train or plane or just hailing a cab, do it in style with this interpretation of our hobo, featuring basket-weave embossed vinyl panels contrasted with solid taupe vinyl. Making rush hour a stylish event is what this bag is all about.

TITLE: *Gym Chic Carryall*   **STUDENT:** Elise Pereira   **PATTERN:** Jamba Gym Bag

With gyms popping up all over the place and everyone looking to stretch and tone themselves, chances are you are one of those people. But, unlike the "pack," you look to be different and distinct. The perfect solution, this gym bag features embossed snakeskin vinyl and solid vinyl body with chartreuse vinyl contrasting handles and detailing. No one will ever accuse you of being part of the masses with this chic carryall.

TITLE: *Tropicana*   **STUDENT:** Nichole Siegfried   **PATTERN:** Diamond Plate Shopping Tote

On the beach, by the pool, or just lounging in your favorite tropical hideaway, this multicolored coated fabric tote with inlaid flowers and leaves and accented with brass grommets is sure to put you in the mood for steel bands and drinks with umbrellas.

TITLE: *Bam Boo Baby* **STUDENT:** Sarah Sylvester **PATTERN:** Retro Sparkle Messenger Bag

What has a black urethane body with silver and green coated fabric appliqué? The Bam Boo Baby, of course. This sophisticated messenger bag has all it takes to hit the mark on fashion. It's soft and lightweight with just the right touches of color and style—perfect for the office or an outing to visit your favorite "animals" at the zoo.

TITLE: *I See Spots*   **STUDENT:** Debbie Yehaskel   **PATTERN:** Diamond Plate Shopping Tote

When you need the perfect accessory to coordinate with your entire wardrobe, turn to this interpretation of our shopping tote. Made of woven fabric and sporting a clear plastic handle and inlays of colored spots, this bag is sure to catch the eye of all your friends. And don't forget the coordinated detachable change purse, perfect for all the important items such as—well you know what they are!

TITLE: *Bazooka Joe Belt*   **STUDENT:** Ashlie Andrews   **PATTERN:** Candy Wrapper Bling Belt

Jazz up your jeans with this easy and eye-catching belt made of vinyl with an inlay of Bazooka Joe bubble gum comics. This belt is the perfect accessory for any member of your family or for that special someone who loves nostalgia.

TITLE: *Tag Bag*   **STUDENT:** Allison Van Hook   **PATTERN:** The 8:08 Express Hobo Bag

Tag, you're it in this gold metallic vinyl hobo with multiprint patches, black plastic chain, and contrasting plastic zipper. This bag is a winner for all occasions.

TITLE: *Lace It Up!*   **STUDENT:** Allison Van Hook   **PATTERN:** Indianapolis Speedway Hobo Bag

It's all about lacing in this shocking pink patent vinyl hobo featuring black plastic chain, licorice-color lacing, and accented with gold plastic lacing in the front. This bag takes on a flower petal look that is sure to blossom into something any fashionista must have in her wardrobe.

Section Four: Patterns

Diamond Plate Shopping Tote Front and Back

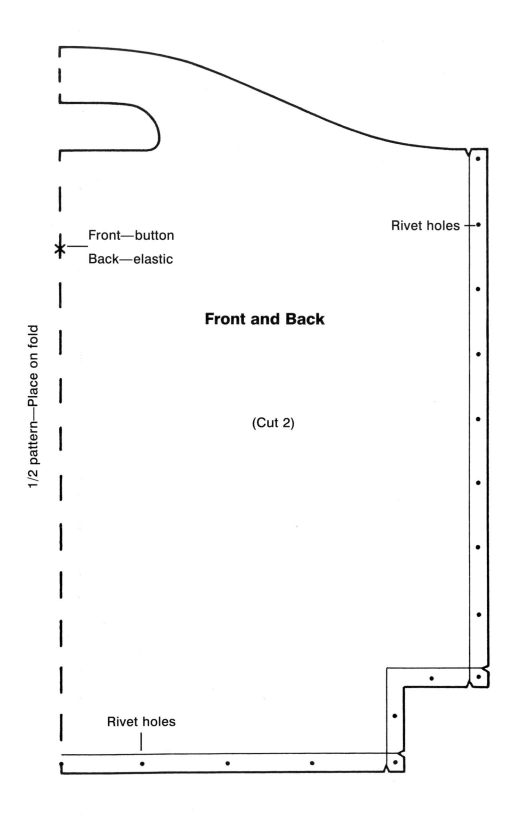

Front—button
Back—elastic

1/2 pattern—Place on fold

Rivet holes

Front and Back

(Cut 2)

Rivet holes

Photocopy at 200%

Kauai Tote Handle

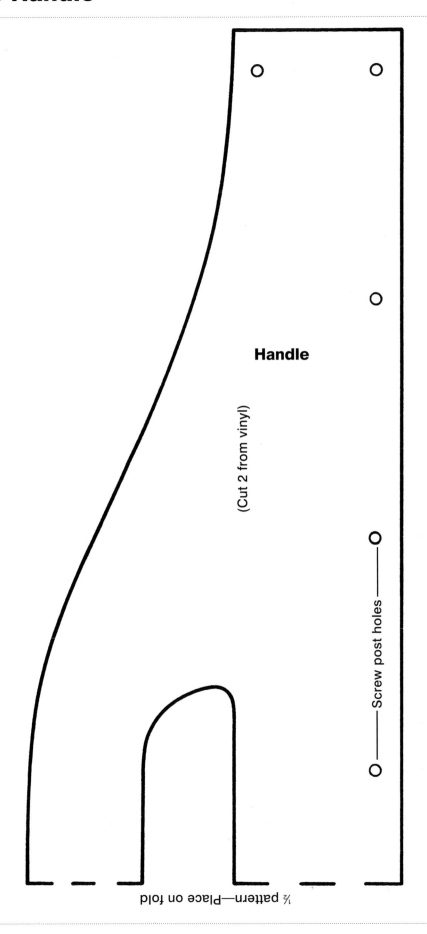

Handle

(Cut 2 from vinyl)

Screw post holes

½ pattern—Place on fold

Kauai Tote Front and Back

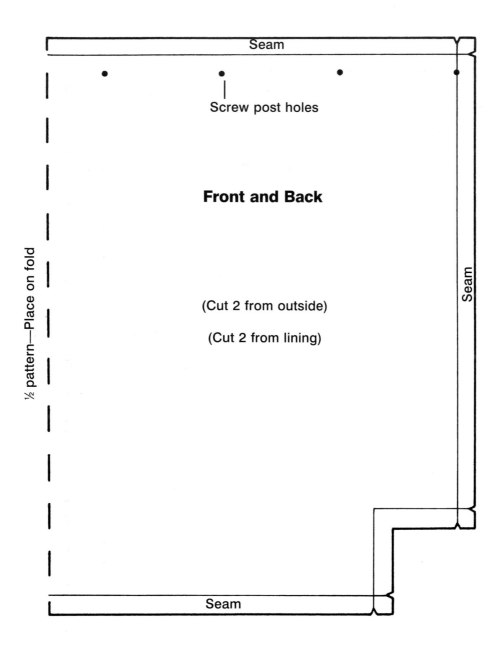

Seam

Screw post holes

Front and Back

(Cut 2 from outside)

(Cut 2 from lining)

½ pattern—Place on fold

Seam

Seam

Kauai Tote Pocket

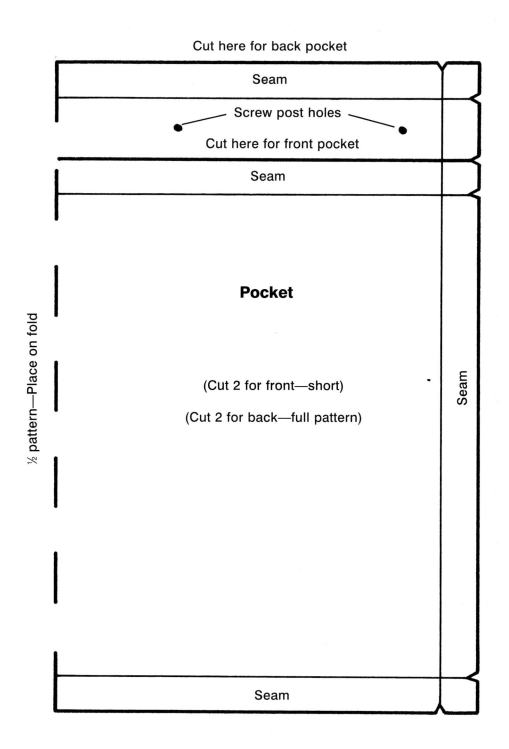

Cut here for back pocket

Seam

Screw post holes

Cut here for front pocket

Seam

½ pattern—Place on fold

Pocket

(Cut 2 for front—short)

(Cut 2 for back—full pattern)

Seam

Seam

Photocopy at 200%

Indianapolis Speedway Hobo Bag Sections 1 & 2 —Left and Right

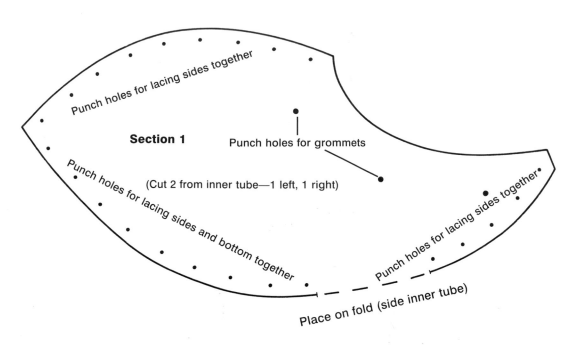

Punch holes for lacing sides together

Section 1

Punch holes for grommets

(Cut 2 from inner tube—1 left, 1 right)

Punch holes for lacing sides and bottom together

Punch holes for lacing sides together

Place on fold (side inner tube)

Photocopy at 200%

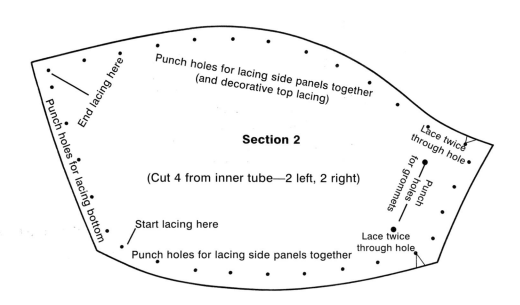

Punch holes for lacing side panels together
(and decorative top lacing)

End lacing here

Punch holes for lacing bottom

Lace twice through hole

Punch holes for grommets

Section 2

(Cut 4 from inner tube—2 left, 2 right)

Start lacing here

Lace twice through hole

Punch holes for lacing side panels together

Photocopy at 200%

Indianapolis Speedway Hobo Bag Section 3—Center Panel

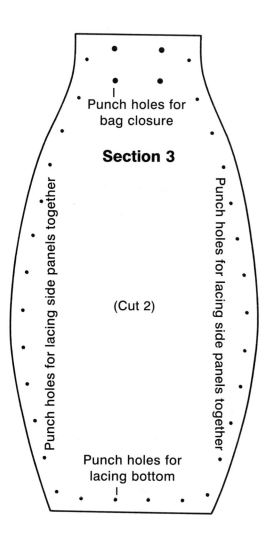

Punch holes for
bag closure

Section 3

Punch holes for lacing side panels together

Punch holes for lacing side panels together

(Cut 2)

Punch holes for
lacing bottom

Photocopy at 200%

The 8:08 Express Hobo Bag Section 1—Left and Right

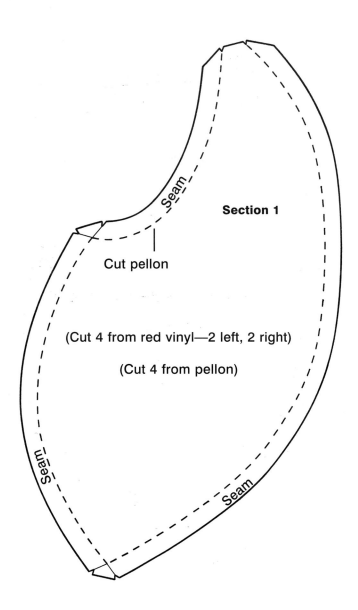

Seam

Cut pellon

Section 1

(Cut 4 from red vinyl—2 left, 2 right)

(Cut 4 from pellon)

Seam

Seam

Photocopy at 200%

The 8:08 Express Hobo Bag Section 2—Left and Right

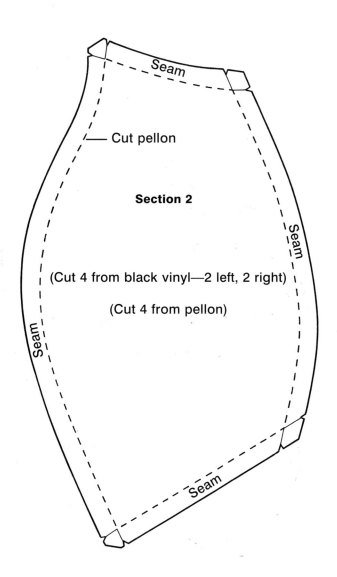

Seam

Cut pellon

Section 2

Seam

(Cut 4 from black vinyl—2 left, 2 right)

(Cut 4 from pellon)

Seam

Seam

Photocopy at 200%

The 8:08 Express Hobo Bag Section 3—Center

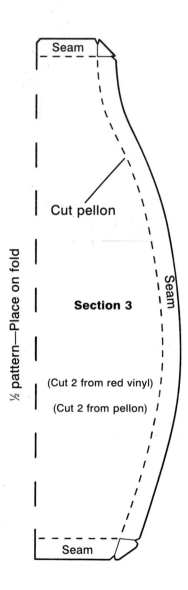

Photocopy at 200%

The 8:08 Express Hobo Bag Lining

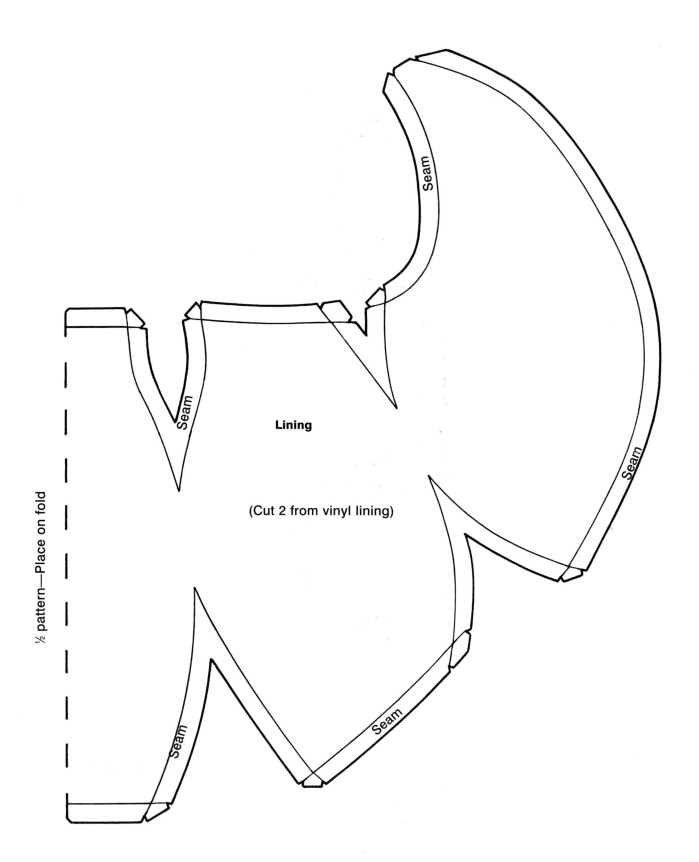

½ pattern—Place on fold

Seam

Seam

Seam

Seam

Seam

Seam

Lining

(Cut 2 from vinyl lining)

Photocopy at 200%

The 8:08 Express Hobo Bag Outside Handle

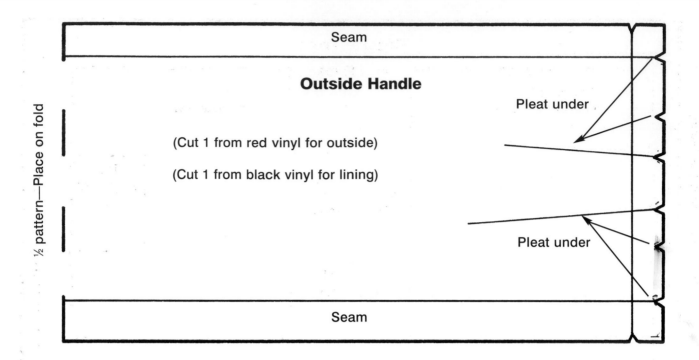

Seam

Outside Handle

½ pattern—Place on fold

(Cut 1 from red vinyl for outside)

(Cut 1 from black vinyl for lining)

Pleat under

Pleat under

Seam

The 8:08 Express Hobo Bag Outside Tabs & Tab Interfacing

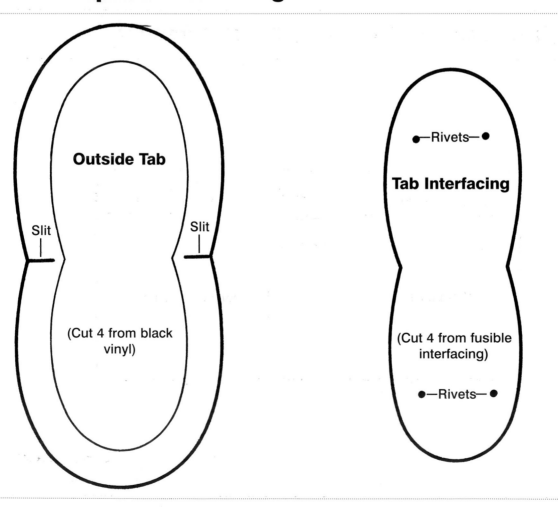

Outside Tab

Slit   Slit

(Cut 4 from black vinyl)

Tab Interfacing

●—Rivets—●

(Cut 4 from fusible interfacing)

●—Rivets—●

Holographic Techno-Wallet Outside Front and Back

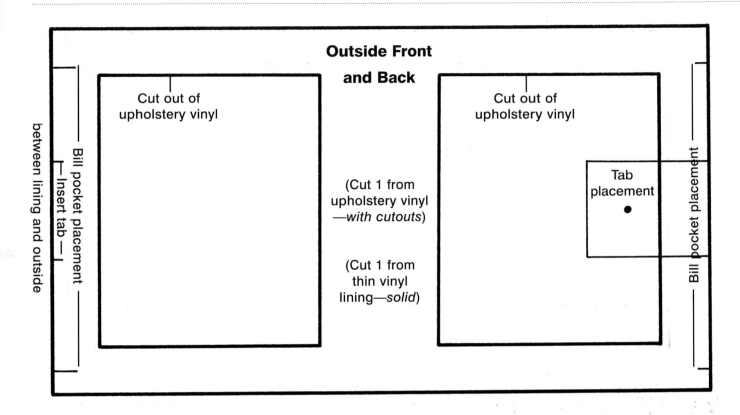

Outside Front and Back

Cut out of upholstery vinyl

Cut out of upholstery vinyl

(Cut 1 from upholstery vinyl —*with cutouts*)

(Cut 1 from thin vinyl lining—*solid*)

Tab placement

Bill pocket placement —Insert tab—

between lining and outside

Bill pocket placement

Holographic Techno-Wallet Interior Bill Pocket

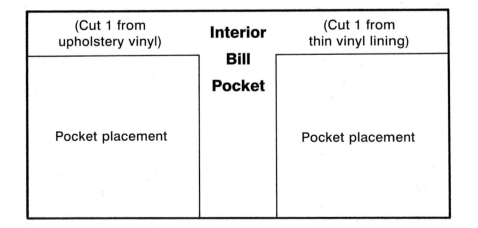

(Cut 1 from upholstery vinyl)

Interior Bill Pocket

(Cut 1 from thin vinyl lining)

Pocket placement

Pocket placement

Photocopy at 200%

Techno-Wallet Holographic Inlay & Interior Side Pocket

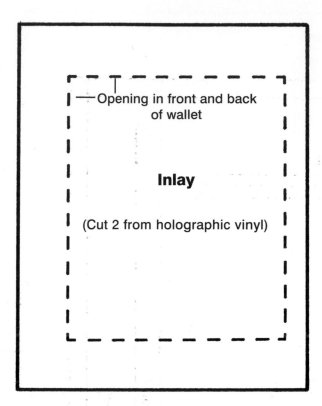

—Opening in front and back of wallet

Inlay

(Cut 2 from holographic vinyl)

Inlay

Interior Side Pocket

(Cut 2 from holographic vinyl)

(Cut 2 from thin vinyl lining)

Interior Side pocket

Techno-Wallet Tab & Holographic Tab Detail

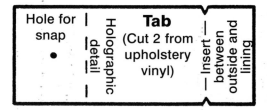

Hole for snap

Holographic detail

Tab
(Cut 2 from upholstery vinyl)

Insert between outside and lining

Detail
(Cut 1 from holographic vinyl)

Nine-to-Five Messenger Bag Front and Back

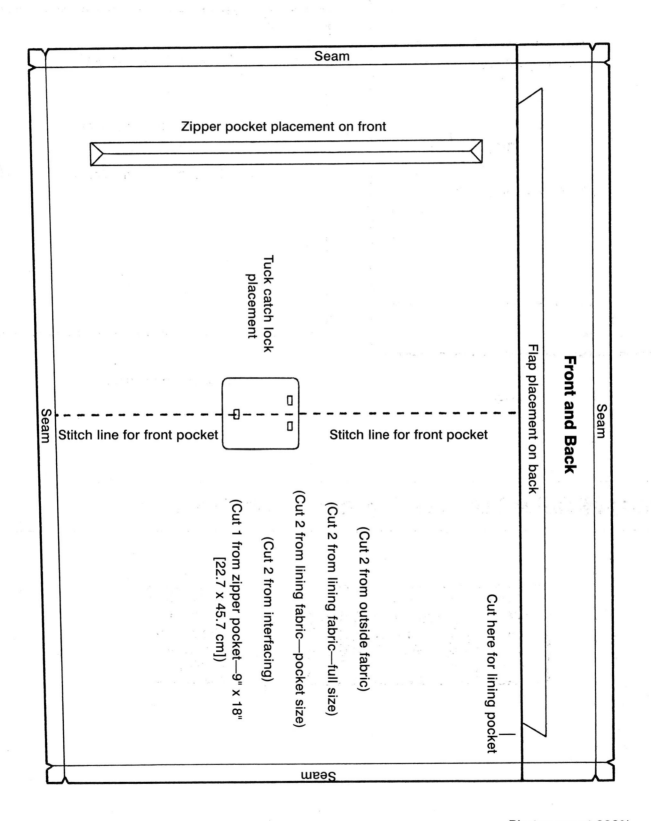

Seam

Zipper pocket placement on front

Tuck catch lock placement

Stitch line for front pocket

Stitch line for front pocket

Seam

Front and Back

Flap placement on back

Cut here for lining pocket

(Cut 2 from outside fabric)

(Cut 2 from lining fabric—full size)

(Cut 2 from lining fabric—pocket size)

(Cut 2 from interfacing)

(Cut 1 from zipper pocket—9" x 18" [22.7 x 45.7 cm])

Seam

Seam

Photocopy at 200%

Nine-to-Five Messenger Bag Outside Flap

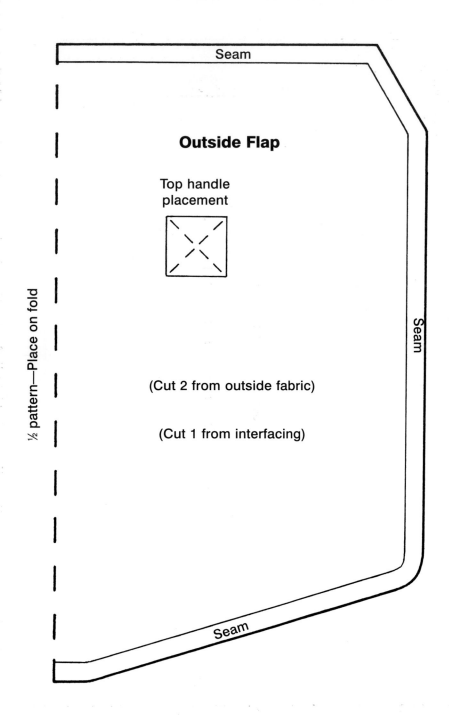

Seam

Outside Flap

Top handle
placement

½ pattern—Place on fold

Seam

(Cut 2 from outside fabric)

(Cut 1 from interfacing)

Seam

Photocopy at 200%

Nine-to-Five Messenger Bag Outside Bottom

½ pattern—Place on fold

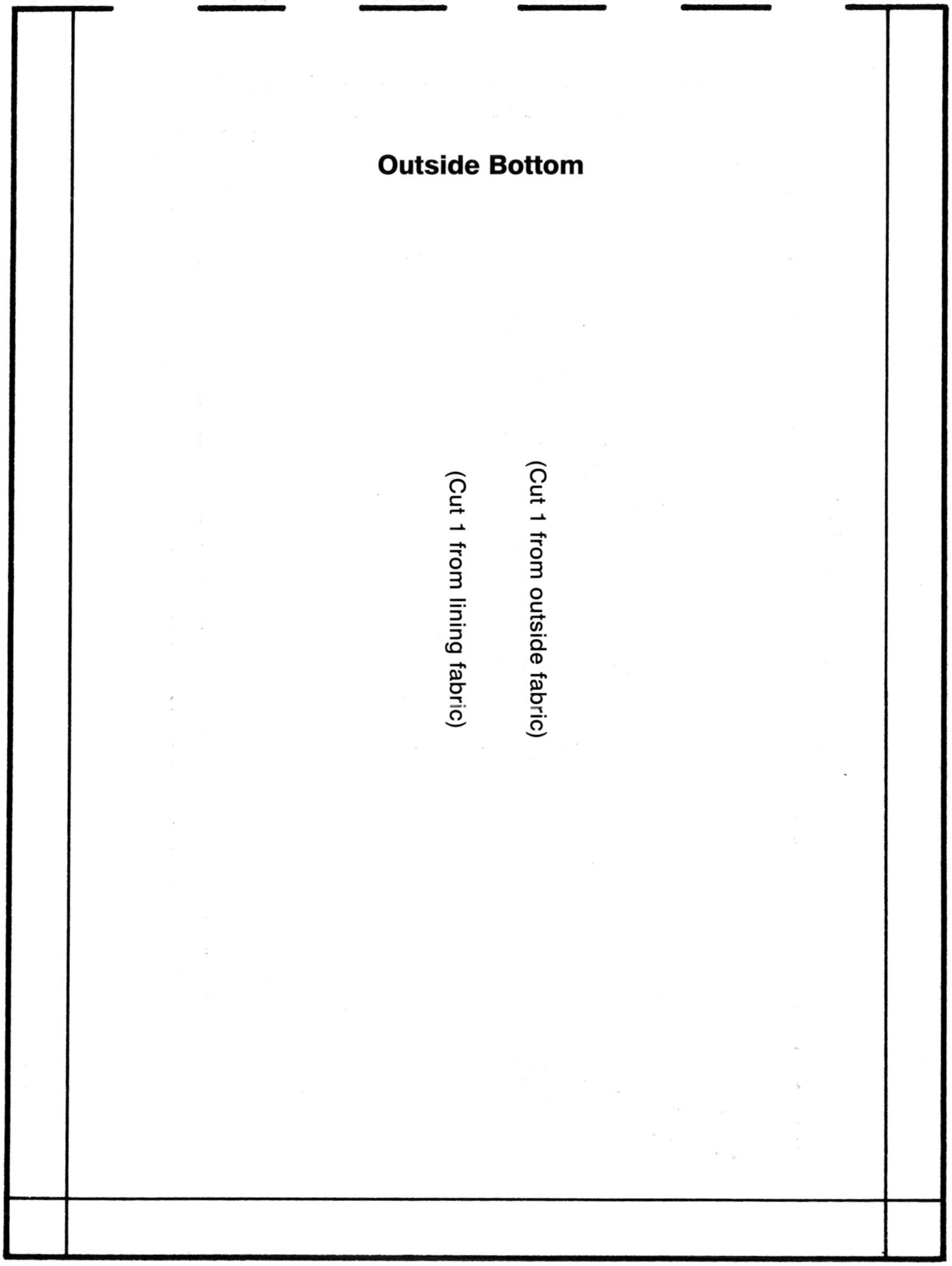

Outside Bottom

(Cut 1 from outside fabric)

(Cut 1 from lining fabric)

Nine-to-Five Messenger Bag Bottom Stay

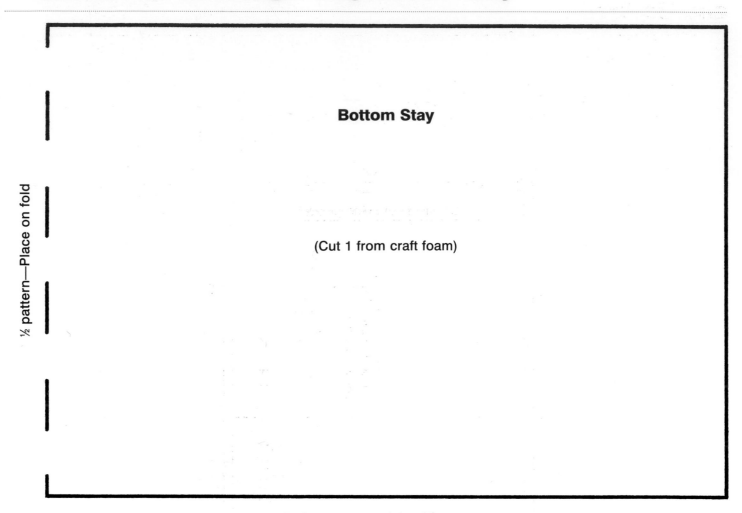

Bottom Stay

(Cut 1 from craft foam)

½ pattern—Place on fold

Nine-to-Five Messenger Bag Outside Gusset

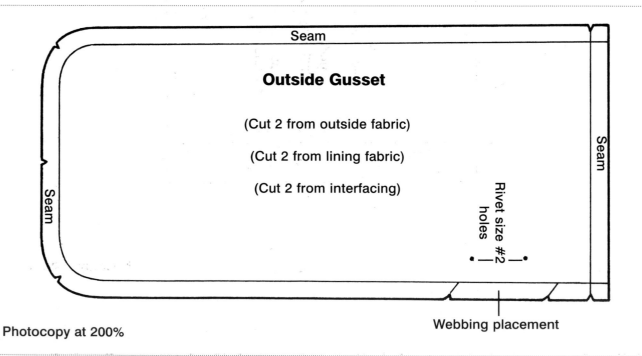

Seam

Outside Gusset

(Cut 2 from outside fabric)

(Cut 2 from lining fabric)

(Cut 2 from interfacing)

Seam

Seam

Rivet size #2 holes

Webbing placement

Photocopy at 200%

Retro Sparkle Messenger Bag Outside Front, Back, and Bottom

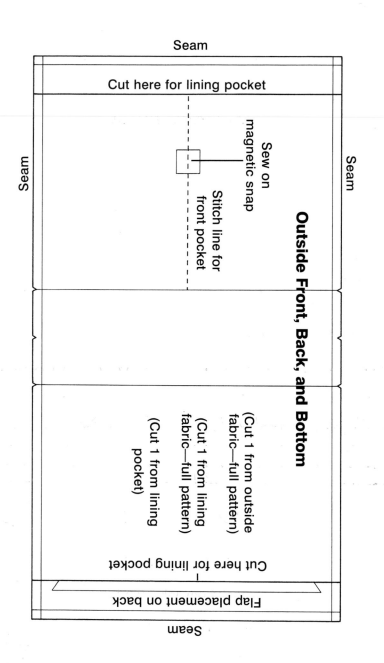

Photocopy at 400%

Retro Sparkle Messenger Bag Outside Flap & Bag Flap Appliqué

½ pattern—Place on fold

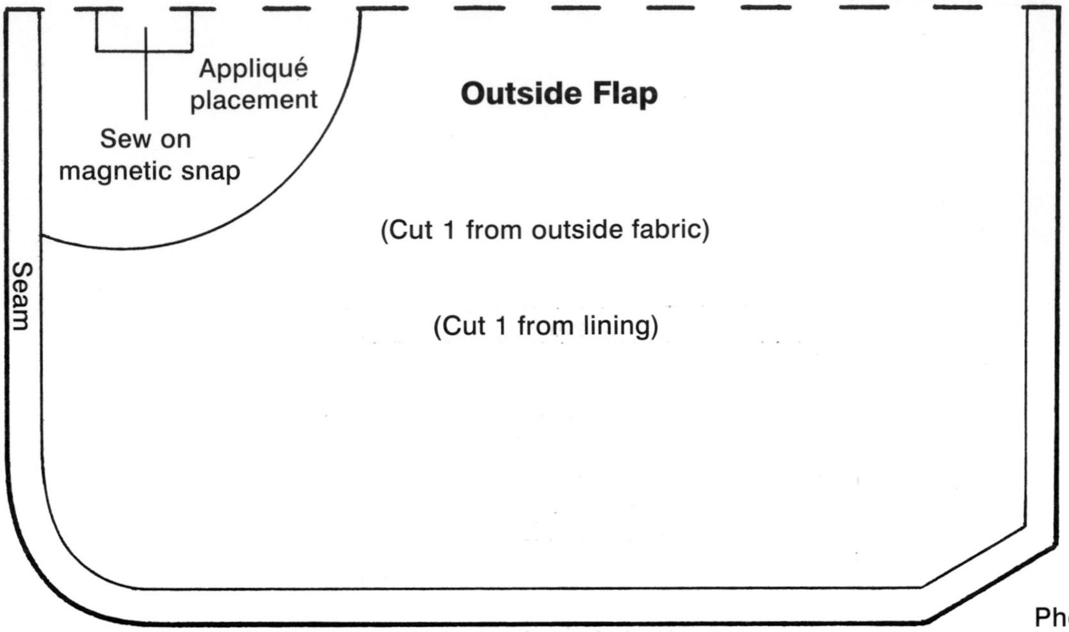

Appliqué placement

Sew on magnetic snap

Seam

Outside Flap

(Cut 1 from outside fabric)

(Cut 1 from lining)

Photocopy at 200%

Flap Appliqué

(Cut 2 from appliqué fabric)

*Cement together first, then cut

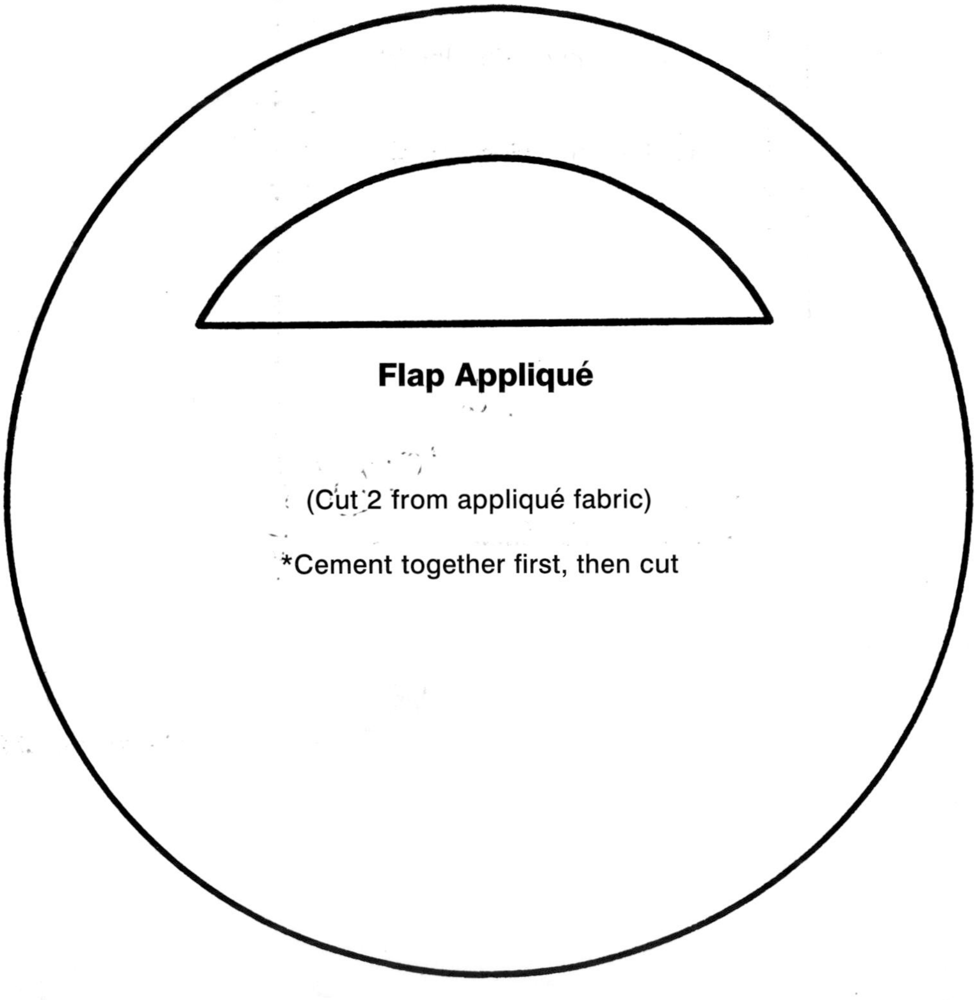

Retro Sparkle Messenger Bag Outside Gusset

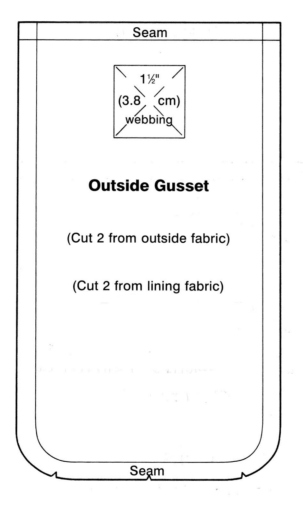

Seam

1½"
(3.8 cm)
webbing

Outside Gusset

(Cut 2 from outside fabric)

(Cut 2 from lining fabric)

Seam

Photocopy at 200%

Aloha Vanity Case Front and Back

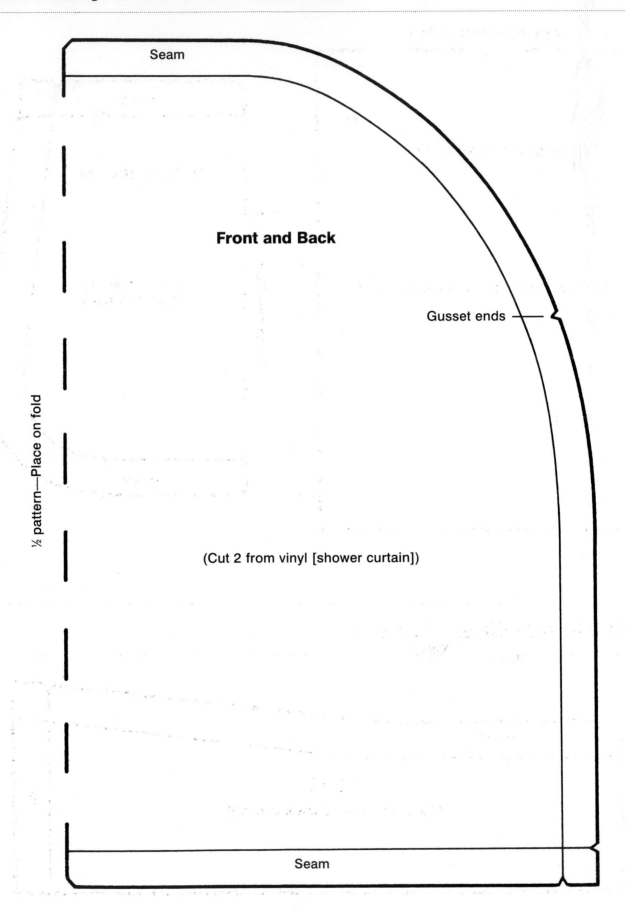

Seam

Front and Back

Gusset ends

½ pattern—Place on fold

(Cut 2 from vinyl [shower curtain])

Seam

Aloha Vanity Case Bottom Reinforcement & Outside Gusset

½ pattern—Place on fold

Bottom Reinforcement

(Cut 1 from medium-/heavyweight vinyl)

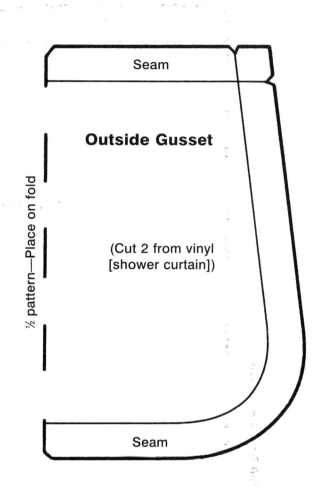

Seam

Outside Gusset

½ pattern—Place on fold

(Cut 2 from vinyl
[shower curtain])

Seam

Aloha Vanity Case Top Zip

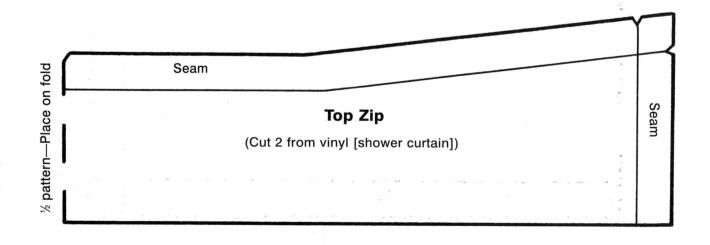

Seam

½ pattern—Place on fold

Seam

Top Zip

(Cut 2 from vinyl [shower curtain])

Jamba Gym Bag Outside Front and Back

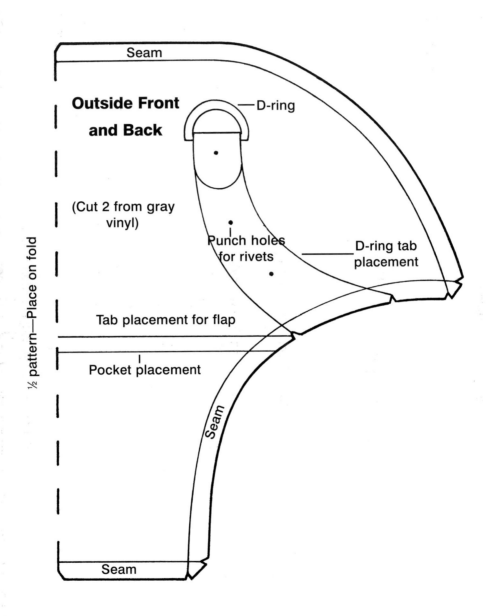

Seam

**Outside Front
and Back**

D-ring

(Cut 2 from gray
vinyl)

Punch holes
for rivets

D-ring tab
placement

½ pattern—Place on fold

Tab placement for flap

Pocket placement

Seam

Seam

Photocopy at 400%

Jamba Gym Bag Outside/Lining Bottom

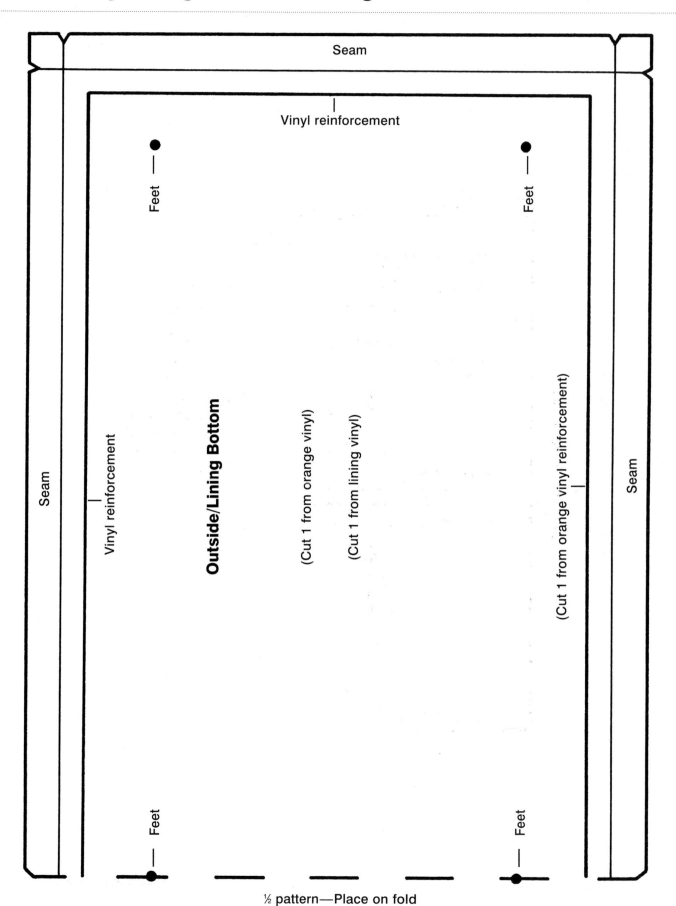

Seam

Vinyl reinforcement

● Feet

Feet ●

Vinyl reinforcement

Seam

Outside/Lining Bottom

(Cut 1 from orange vinyl)

(Cut 1 from lining vinyl)

(Cut 1 from orange vinyl reinforcement)

Seam

Feet

Feet

½ pattern—Place on fold

Jamba Gym Bag Outside/Lining Top Zip

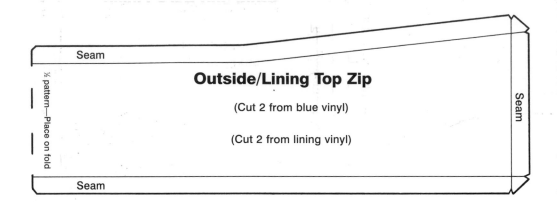

Outside/Lining Top Zip

(Cut 2 from blue vinyl)

(Cut 2 from lining vinyl)

Seam

½ pattern—Place on fold

Seam

Seam

Photocopy at 200%

Jamba Gym Bag Outside/Lining Side Gusset Panel

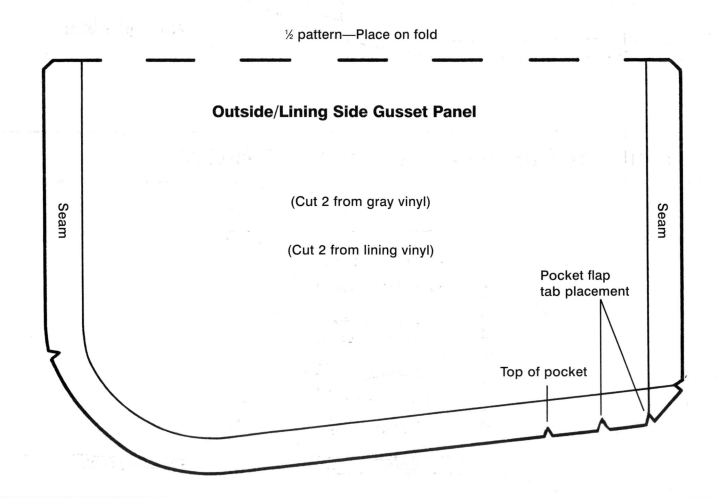

½ pattern—Place on fold

Outside/Lining Side Gusset Panel

(Cut 2 from gray vinyl)

(Cut 2 from lining vinyl)

Seam

Seam

Pocket flap
tab placement

Top of pocket

Jamba Gym Bag Front and Back Lining

½ pattern—Place on fold

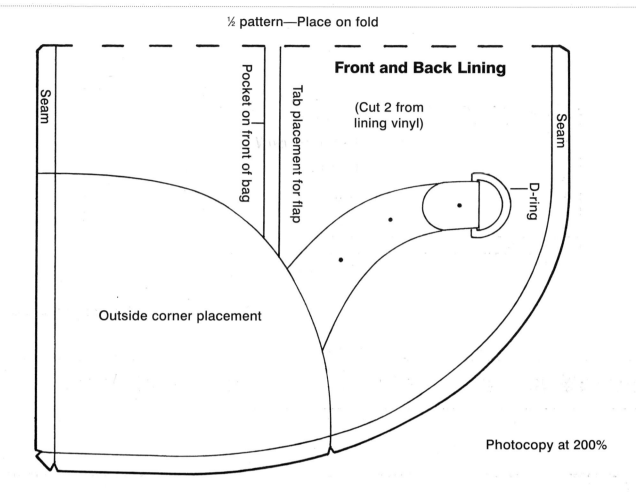

Front and Back Lining

(Cut 2 from lining vinyl)

Seam

Pocket on front of bag

Tab placement for flap

D-ring

Outside corner placement

Photocopy at 200%

Jamba Gym Bag Outside/Lining Front Pocket

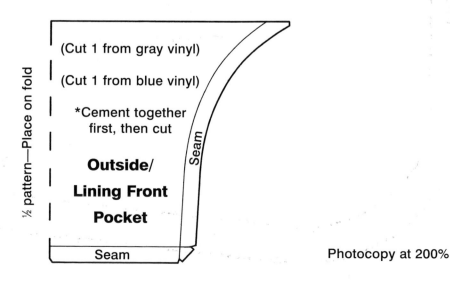

(Cut 1 from gray vinyl)

(Cut 1 from blue vinyl)

*Cement together first, then cut

½ pattern—Place on fold

Seam

Outside/ Lining Front Pocket

Seam

Photocopy at 200%

Jamba Gym Bag Outside/Lining Side Pocket

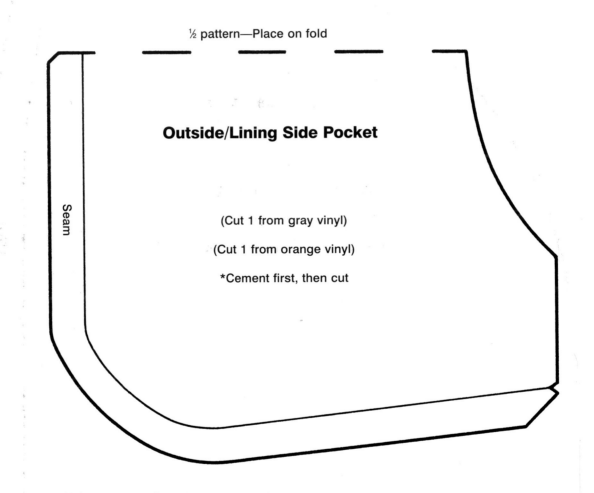

½ pattern—Place on fold

Outside/Lining Side Pocket

(Cut 1 from gray vinyl)

(Cut 1 from orange vinyl)

*Cement first, then cut

Seam

Jamba Gym Bag Outside Corner

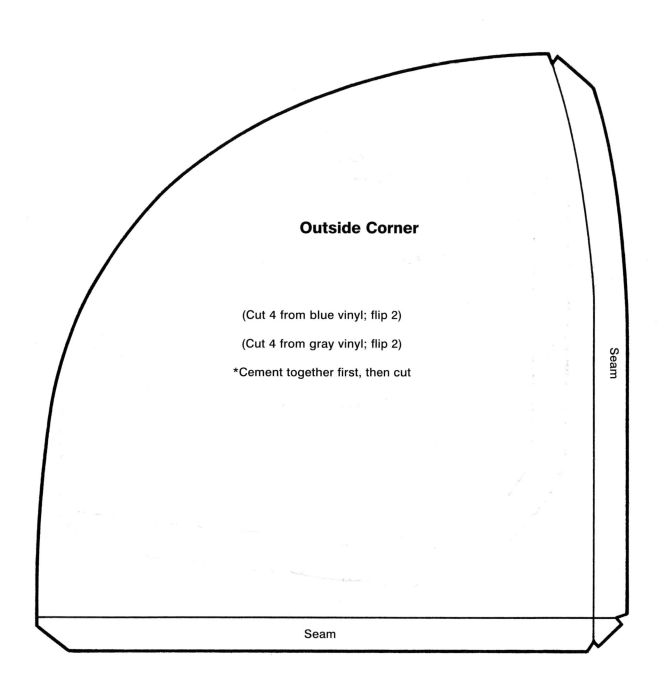

Outside Corner

(Cut 4 from blue vinyl; flip 2)

(Cut 4 from gray vinyl; flip 2)

*Cement together first, then cut

Seam

Seam

Jamba Gym Bag Outside/Lining Side Pocket Flap

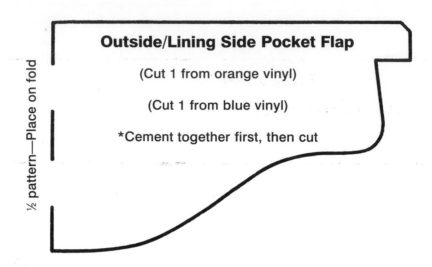

Outside/Lining Side Pocket Flap

(Cut 1 from orange vinyl)

(Cut 1 from blue vinyl)

*Cement together first, then cut

½ pattern—Place on fold

Jamba Gym Bag Outside/Lining D-ring Tab

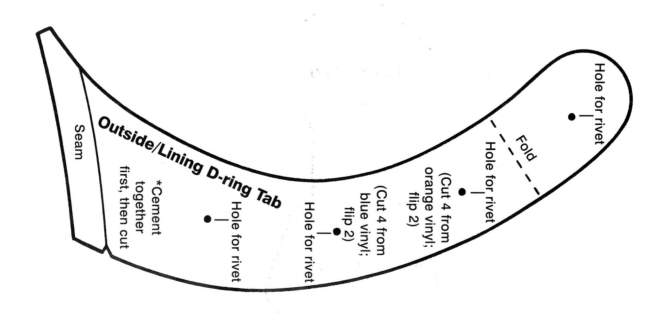

Seam

Outside/Lining D-ring Tab

*Cement together first, then cut

Hole for rivet

Hole for rivet

(Cut 4 from blue vinyl; flip 2)

Hole for rivet

(Cut 4 from orange vinyl; flip 2)

Hole for rivet

Fold

Hole for rivet

Jamba Gym Bag Outside Handle

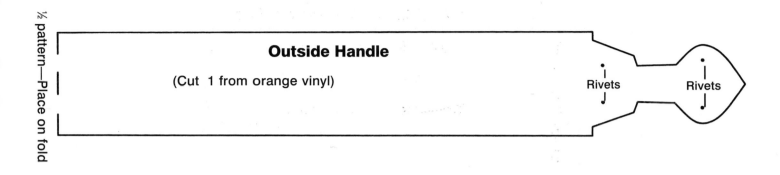

½ pattern—Place on fold

Outside Handle

(Cut 1 from orange vinyl)

Rivets   Rivets

Photocopy at 200%

Jamba Gym Bag Handle End

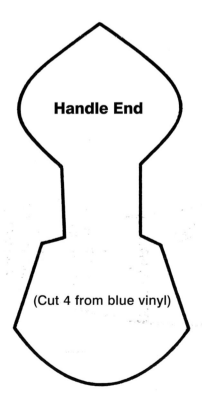

Handle End

(Cut 4 from blue vinyl)

Contributors

Ashlie Andrews
ashlie_andrews@fitnyc.edu
87

Charles Christen
charles_christen@fitnyc.edu
72

Shara Cohn
shara_cohn@fitnyc.edu
73

JoAnne Espinell
joanne_espinell@fitnyc.edu
74

Angela Finochio
ngcangel@optonline.net
75

Jennifer Hall
jlh827@hotmail.com
76

Jessica Hymowitz
jessicouture@aol.com
79

Maria Napolitano
maria_napolitano@fitnyc.edu
77

Stefani Oblak
stefani_oblak@fitnyc.edu
78

Shelley Parker
inmyshoes@nyc.rr.com
80, 81

Elise Pereira
elisemarie126@yahoo.com
82, 83

Nichole Siegfried
anticrombie74@aol.com
84

Sarah Sylvester
fashongal@comcast.net
85

Allison Van Hook
allison_vanhook@fitnyc.edu
88, 89

Debbie Yehaskel
dyehaskel@yahoo.com
86

Glossary

Appliqué: A cutout decoration fastened to a larger piece of material by sewing, adhesive, or other means, such as rivets.

Binder Clip: Also called "bulldog clips," these strong metal clips are sold in stationery or office supply stores and are for holding large stacks of paper, but they also work well for holding layers of fabric or material together.

Bone Folder: Originally made of bone but now often made of plastic, this tool is used to open and flatten seams or turn edges.

Coated Fabric: Any fabric that has a layer of lacquer, varnish, propylene, rubber, or plastic resin on either one side or both sides. This layer acts as a water repellent and can be used on cotton, silk, and oilcloth.

Embossed: A raised surface pattern on the surface of a material. Embossing is generally used to simulate other exotic animal skins such as alligator, ostrich, or crocodile.

Embroidery Needle: A classic needle with an oversized eye used for sewing embroidery stitches on cloth and other materials.

Eyelet: A small, circular metal ring that is set into a hole primarily designed to receive a cord or used as decoration.

Gauge Foot: A sewing machine presser foot that has an edge guide, which allows you to stitch a predetermined measurement from the needle.

Glover's Needle: An arrowhead-shaped, highly sharp, three-sided needle used for handsewing through or beading on leather and leatherlike materials.

Grommet: A (generally larger) metal eyelet used as decoration or to strengthen and protect an opening. Also used to insulate or protect something passed through it, such as cording or a handle.

Gusset: An insert in the side of a bag to give it depth and expansion.

Impregnated Fabric: Fabric with a coating infused into the weave of the fabric, allowing it to become waterproof. Some impregnated fabrics are cotton canvas or oilcloth.

Interfacing: A common term for a variety of materials used on the unseen or "wrong" side of fabrics in sewing. Interfacings can be used to stiffen or add body to fabric, to strengthen a certain area of the fabric, or to keep fabrics from stretching out of shape. Interfacings come in a variety of weights and stiffnesses to suit different purposes. Most modern interfacings are made to be ironed in place, though some must still be sewn by hand or machine.

Lacing Needle: A flat needle with a wedge-type device at the eye for gripping the lace.

Lining: Fabric or a lightweight material used for the inside of the bag. It can be the same color as the outside of the bag or a contrasting color for more visual interest.

Pinking: A V-shaped edge made by using pinking shears to cut a serrated edge at a seam to prevent fabric from unraveling. Also used as a decorative edge on fabrics and leathers.

Quilting: The effect obtained by stitching, either by hand or machine, two or more layers of fabric together with padding in between. The stitching can be a geometric pattern or a decorative design.

Reverse Appliqué or Inlay: The ability to add color and shape through cutwork. Contrasting colored material is placed under surface material that has been cut out to resemble a shape, flower, or animal.

Rotary Cutter: A tool with a round blade, resembling a pizza cutter, used for cutting straight lines on fabric.

(continued)

Glossary *(continued)*

Rubberized Fabric: Defined by the FTC (Federal Trade Commission) as "a manufactured fiber in which the fiber-forming substance is composed of natural or synthetic rubber," rubberized fabric is similar to an *impregnated* fabric. There is a wide range of rubberized fabrics including cotton, rainwear, and shower curtains, many of which feature prints and patterns.

Silk-screened: A fabric that has a printed decorative design motif added to the surface.

Smocking: A hand-stitching technique that secures the pleats or folds of the material.

Stay-Stitch: A stitch technique added to a simple layer of fabric to stabilize it and prevent distortion.

Suede: A finish that has been added to synthetic fabrics to create a buffed or brushed suedelike surface.

Teflon Foot: A sewing machine presser foot (either made entirely of Teflon or Teflon coated) used to sew leather, suede, and other material.

Thermoplastic: A type of plastic resin that is formed into fibers and then fabricated into cloth. A clear plastic tablecloth or shower curtain would be made of this type of material. Thermoplastics have a tendency to be more brittle and less pliable than urethanes or coated fabrics.

Topstitching: A stitch that is seen on the outside of a project, oftentimes decorative stitching used to add detailing to a sewing project. It is often done in a contrasting thread color.

Trapunto: A decorative quilted or padded design in high relief that is worked through at least two layers of material by gluing and/or outlining the design in running stitch and padding it from the underside.

Urethane: A general term for a versatile synthetic material that can be firm, flexible, or liquid, depending on the manufacturing process. Urethane fabrics can be embossed to resemble leathers, snakeskin, and other exotic skins.

Vinyl: A general term for a material made of polymers or polyvinyl chloride. Vinyl can come in a variety of colors and textures. It is extremely durable and, in some cases, can be handled the same way as leather.

Zipper Foot: A single-toed presser foot that is notched on both sides to accommodate the needle and to facilitate stitching a zipper.

Resources

A.C. Moore
www.acmoore.com
Nationwide locations
(Arts and crafts supplies)

Active Trimming Co.
250 West 39th Street
New York, NY 10018 USA
800.878.6336
(Trimmings and notions)

Atlanta Thread & Supply Co.
695 Red Oak Road
Stockbridge, GA 30281 USA
800.847.1001
store.atlantathread.com
(Notions)
Catalog available

Beacon Fabric & Notions
8331 Epicenter Boulevard
Lakeland, FL 33809 USA
800.713.8157
www.beaconfabric.com
(Fabrics and notions)

Brewer Sewing Supplies
3800 West 42nd Street
Chicago, IL 60632 USA
800.444.3111
www.brewersewing.com
(Sewing supplies)

C.S. Osborne & Co.
125 Jersey Street
Harrison, NJ 07029 USA
973.483.3232
www.csosborne.com
(Tools)
Catalog available

Canal Plastics Center
345 Canal Street
New York, NY 10013 USA
212.925.1666
www.canalplasticscenter.com
(Plastics)

Canal Rubber
329 Canal Street
New York, NY 10013 USA
800.444.6483
www.canalrubber.com
(Rubber)

Charm Woven Labels
2400 West Magnolia Boulevard
Burbank, CA 91506 USA
800.843.1111
www.charmwoven.com
(Woven labels)
Catalog available

Denver Fabrics
2777 West Belleview
Littleton, CO 80123 USA
866.996.4573
www.denverfabrics.com
(Fabrics and notions)

The Fabric and Fiber Sourcebook
Published by Threads Magazine
Mail-order guide available through
www.amazon.com and
www.barnesandnoble.com

Great Lakes Fabrics, Inc.
1904 South Wenona Street
Bay City, MI 48706 USA
800.652.2358
www.glfi.com
(Fabrics and notions)

Hansol Sewing Machine Co., Inc.
101 West 26th Street
New York, NY 10001 USA
800.463.9661
(Sewing machines)

Herrschners
2800 Hoover Road
Stevens Point, WI 54492 USA
800.441.0838
www.herrschners.com
(Sewing and craft supplies, fabrics)
Catalog available

HobbyCraft Canada
905.738.6556
www.hobbycraft.com
(Craft supplies)

HobbyCraft Group Limited
7 Enterprise Way
Aviation Park
Bournemouth International Airport
Christchurch
Dorset BH23 6HG UK
+44.01202.596100
www.hobbycraft.co.uk
(Craft supplies)

Jo-Ann Fabric & Crafts
888.739.4120
www.joann.com
Nationwide locations
(Craft supplies, fabrics, and trimmings)
Catalog and magazine available

Resources *(continued)*

M & J Trimming
1008 6th Avenue
New York, NY 10018 USA
800.965.8746
www.mjtrim.com
(Trimmings)

Michael's Arts & Crafts
800.642.4235
www.michaels.com
Nationwide locations
(Arts and crafts supplies)

Pearl Paint
800.451.7327
www.pearlpaint.com
Nationwide locations
(Craft supplies)
Catalog available

Seattle Fabrics
8702 Aurora Avenue North
Seattle, WA 98103 USA
866.925.0670
www.seattlefabrics.com
(Fabrics and notions)

Siegel of California
700 McMurray Road
Buellton, CA 93427 USA
800.862.8956
www.siegelofca.com
(Tools and notions)

Sommers Plastic Products Co., Inc.
PO Box 4356
31 Styertowne Road
Clifton, NJ 07012 USA
800.225.7677
www.sommers.com
(Plastics, vinyl, and coated fabrics)

Universal Mercantile Exchange, Inc.
21128 Commerce Point Drive
Walnut, CA 91789 USA
800.755.6608
www.umei.com
(Buckles, buttons, chains, fasteners,
handles, ornaments, and trims)
Catalog available

Henry Westpfal & Co.
107 West 30th Street
New York, NY 10001 USA
212.563.5990
(Tools)
Catalog available

About the Authors

Ellen Goldstein-Lynch (left) is the chairperson of the accessories design department at the Fashion Institute of Technology in New York City. She has been involved in the accessories field for more than 25 years and has served as public relations director for the National Fashion Accessories Association for 10 years. She is an authority on handbags and accessories and has been featured on national television and in print.

Nicole Malone (right) is an accessories designer with a passion for handbags. Originally Brooklyn based, she now lives in the outskirts of Baltimore, Maryland. Her past freelance experience includes pattern making, sample making, and making custom, one-of-a-kind creations for various handbag and fashion designers. A graduate of the Accessories Design Program at the Fashion Institute of Technology, she currently designs and produces her own line of handbags and belts, but her true love is teaching the students in the Accessories Design Department at her alma mater.

Sarah Mullins (center) is a graduate and faculty member of the accessories design department at the Fashion Institute of Technology. Sarah does freelance design for several New York City–based companies and also has her own line of unique handbags. Her passion is experimenting with different combinations of materials in her designs.

Ellen Goldstein-Lynch, Sarah Mullins, and Nicole Malone coauthored their best-selling first book, *Making Handbags: Retro, Chic, Luxurious* (Rockport, 2002), and its follow-up, *Making Leather Handbags and Other Stylish Accessories* (Quarry, 2004).

Photo: Ilan Schwarz & VASÍLIOS

Acknowledgments

To Jim, Thomas, Janis, Brandon, Larry, Jess, Evan, and Dennis, you guys totally rock my world! Thanks for your continued dedication, love, and support. To "Uncle B," my inspiration; I will keep you in my heart forever. And, to Gale Keenan, "buds forever."

Thanks to Mary Ann and the Quarry wizards for pitching this book and the other two. To my coauthors Sarah and Nicole, thanks for letting me be as creative with words as you guys are with bags. You never cease to amaze me! To Drs. John Marino and Elisa Port; without you, I would not be here today! To the faculty, staff, and students of the accessories design department, thank you for making my life at FIT worthwhile. And to our readers, thanks for the challenge!

—**Ellen Goldstein-Lynch**

So many people to thank, so little room! It's been a bit of a rough year for me, and when times are tough, that's when I realize how truly blessed I am for having wonderful friends and family. Mommy and Daddy, you have always supported me, no matter what; I love you so much and I don't know where I'd be without you! Peter, Patti, Shannon, and Erin—I love you Shnozzies! Sarah, you're such a great friend who still always keeps me sane, and Shelley, you keep me sane too, but it's fun when you let me get insane on occasion! Julie, you're always there for me, and you make me feel relatively sane. And Brian, across the miles, the love is always right there. The faculty at FIT who have taught me so much, and especially Ellen, I admire you for always "getting it done," but always taking time out to listen and be supportive. Eternal thanks to my students, who are always the light of my day; they are the reason that I do what I do. To Westside Crew, thanks for always dealing with me; it's something that's always appreciated! Mary Ann and the wonderful people at Quarry Books, what an amazing experience, once again, for the third time around! Shooky, you're my fluffy, nasty little muse. To Dad Malone and the memory of Mom Malone, who was such a wonderful person and someone who is so deeply missed; you will always be an inspiration of the type of person I would like to be one day. And finally to Kevin, for the support you have given me; it means everything knowing that you're here for me and that we'll always have each other. I love you always.

—**Nicole Malone**

Thank you to all of the people in my life who give me their love and support. My two favorite guys, Alex and Oliver, get the most gratitude for bearing with me during the writing of this book. Thank you to my family, Mom, Dad, Amy, and Tina; you are the roots of my confidence and creativity. Thank you to Maureen for keeping me up to date on the world at large and always looking great with a handbag. Nicole and Shelley, you two are a constant source of amusement and great ideas. All of you Brooklynites deserve credit too: Lasley and Andrew, Meg, Dan, Scott, Josh, Holly, J. D. and Kathy, and the Oslo clan. To the faculty, staff, and students of the FIT accessories design department, you all make learning exciting. Thank you to Nicole, who speaks the same handbag language, Ellen, who always supports me, and Mary Ann for repeating a third great book-writing experience.

—**Sarah Mullins**